D1235675

TINY
NEW YORK

Well you're in your little room
And you're working on
something good
But if it's really good
You're gonna need a bigger room
And when you're in
the bigger room
You might not know what to do
You might have to think of
How you got started sitting in your
little room.

—THE WHITE STRIPES, *LITTLE ROOM*

TINY

The
Smallest Things
in the
Biggest City

NY

NEW YORK

SUZI SIEGEL

Globe
Pequot
Guilford, Connecticut

Globe Pequot

An imprint of The Rowman & Littlefield Publishing Group, Inc.
4501 Forbes Blvd., Ste. 200
Lanham, MD 20706
www.rowman.com

Distributed by NATIONAL BOOK NETWORK

Unless otherwise noted, photos by Suzi Siegel
Photos on p. 7 © Gabriel Levicky
Photos on p. 18 © Alex Schibli; National Oceanic and Atmospheric Administration
Photos on pp. 46–49 © Little Victory Theatre
Photos on p. 99 © Laura Collins
Photos on pp. 130–133 © New York Yankees
Photo on p. 140 © AMNH/R. Mickens
Photos on pp. 164–167 © The Metropolitan Museum of Art
Photos on pp. 172–178 © Alan Wolfson and Hollis Taggart
Galleries, Photography by Josh Nefsky, NY.
Photos on p. 190 © Leslie Day

British Library Cataloguing in Publication Information available

Library of Congress Cataloging-in-Publication Data available

ISBN 978-1-4930-5045-1 (paperback)
ISBN 978-1-4930-3151-1 (e-book)

♾™ The paper used in this publication meets the minimum requirements
of American National Standard for Information Sciences—Permanence
of Paper for Printed Library Materials, ANSI/NISO Z39.48-1992

ACKNOWLEDGMENTS

To my tinies, Rebecca and David Siegel,
my little sister and brother, whose birth earned me the
title "big" for the first and only time in my life.

To my mom, Linda Navarro,
who always let me know that even if my feet couldn't
touch the ground, I still belonged at the table.

And to the Chicken Hawk,
who relentlessly pursued Foghorn Leghorn, despite
being told it was a fruitless exercise.

Like a great river that runs toward the ocean, the narrowness of discipline leads into the openness of panoramic awareness.

—CHÖGYAM TRUNGPA RINPOCHE,
THE POCKET CHÖGYAM RINPOCHE

CONTENTS

(IN SIZE ORDER FROM
TINY TO TINIEST)

CONTENTS

CONTENTS

CONTENTS

CONTENTS

28

29

30

31

32

33

INTRODUCTION

In a giant city like New York, it's easy to overlook the tiny things. New York may be famous for its towering skyscrapers and colossal neon billboards, but it's actually the little things that tell the real New York story. And if you go poking around in the city's smallest nooks and crannies, you find out Tiny isn't what you thought it was.

Because, in New York, Tiny isn't cute. It's tough. Tiny doesn't wait for handouts. It hustles. Tiny isn't insignificant. It's precise. Tiny isn't a jack-of-all-trades. It's the master of one.

Take the West Fourth Street Courts in the Village (a.k.a. "The Cage"). It's half the size of a regulation basketball court, but there's nothing cute about it. The street ball there gets intense, since players have to drive to the basket harder and get the shot off quicker. Twig Terrariums in Williamsburg creates miniature worlds out of moss and tiny

Tiny isn't cute. It's tough.

figurines. Peer into one of their glass jars, though, and you might find a thumbnail-size mobster beating a snitch to death with a baseball bat.

Up in the Bronx, the Yankees' smallest player, Ronald Torreyes, stands only 5 feet 8 inches. But, as a young boy in Venezuela, his dad taught him to work twice as hard as everyone else if he wanted to make it to the big leagues.

The city's tiniest neighborhood, Ramblersville, Queens, was all but forsaken after being decimated by Hurricane Sandy. Yet one ninety-three-year-old lifelong resident turned down the city's payout to relocate and rebuilt her home from the soggy rubble.

OK, truth be told.

But Tiny is not just tough—it's resourceful. Because you have to do more with less when there's so little room to go around—like the yoga teacher in Jackson Heights who got rid of all of her furniture to turn her studio apartment into a yoga studio. Ditto for the guy who lives aboard a houseboat in City Island and has to row to shore for fresh water.

Tiny can

Tiny is also meticulous, because when the canvas is small, there's precious little room for mistakes. The diamond cutter on West 47th Street knows this all too well. As does the tattoo artist in Alphabet City specializing in designs the size of a quarter. Because the thing about Tiny is, it does one thing, and it does it well. People line up around the block at a pocket-size takeout place in Bed-Stuy that has singularly perfected a Trinidadian street food called Doubles. And the teacher coaching immigrants how to pass the taxi test in a cramped basement classroom in Queens isn't called the "Stanley Kaplan of Taxi School" for nothing.

And, OK, truth be told, Tiny can sometimes be cute. But always, always with an edge, because this is New York City. Take Sully, the NYPD's smallest police dog who could not be more adorable. But Sully's got a job to do that is no less than sniffing out terrorism and saving lives. Even the tiniest library, as charming as it is, is not without its grit. Located below ground in a Midtown subway station, it's been known to attract confused commuters who wander in looking to buy a MetroCard.

At the end of the day, New York is a city so immense it can make everyone—natives and visitors alike—feel small. Yet the city's grandest things are actually some of its tiniest. Lucky for all of us, they've managed to eke out a little place for themselves in the greatest city in the world. Because, as crammed together as everything in New York City is, it turns out there's room here for everyone.

sometimes be cute.

1

13TH CONGRESSIONAL DISTRICT
U.S. HOUSE DISTRICT
UPPER MANHATTAN AND WEST BRONX
10¼ SQUARE MILES

Congressman Adriano Espaillat is not only the
first Dominican-American to serve in the House,
he is also the first formerly undocumented
immigrant. His journey from Washington
Heights to Washington D.C. has been about
taking on the entrenched political machine,
and his tiny district is .2 percent the area of
the country's largest one. So it's no surprise to
anyone his priority is fighting for the little guy.

The 13th is one of the largest districts in terms of the population but, geographically, it's one of the smallest. It's very compact. Some members drive for hours and hours through their districts. I have no troubles walking mine on a good day.

"There's no shortage of opinions about whether it's easier to represent a small district or a big one. There's a district in Alaska that's a half a million square miles. Mine is ten. I think mine's easier. Although the compactness also brings challenges—overcrowding, gridlock, traffic. If more people use the same subway station every day, it's like your brake pads. You're gonna have to change them every once in a while.

"It's a very diverse district of spunk. You have an iconic place like Harlem, which is the capital of the African diaspora. Then you have East Harlem—El Barrio—which is the cradle of Latinos with a Puerto Rican presence and history there.

"Then you have Washington Heights and Inwood, which has its own personality. It has its own pulse, its own attitude. It wakes up one day very happy, the next day very grouchy. It's surrounded by beautiful parks, and it's the highest point in Manhattan.

"And then you have the northwest Bronx, which is also a special place—Albanians in Norwood, Vietnamese on University Avenue. You also have West Africans, Puerto Ricans, Dominicans, Mexicans. And some enclaves of Irish and Jewish neighborhoods are still there. That's the district—very exciting and very diverse.

"I have gone up against the establishment many times in my career. Politics are a full contact sport. I have a little bit of a chip on my shoulder. I got a little spunk: I like challenges, and I don't take no for an answer.

"I think anybody who's migrated here had it hard. People like my grandparents, who came in the fifties before the bodegas sold platanos. I always think about how it must have been for them to come here. It takes a kind of innovativeness to be successful when the deck is stacked against you.

"Washington D.C. right now is a roller-coaster ride. But I'm built for the scenario because I fight. I like to challenge, push, throw an elbow if I have to.

"I don't understand the anti-immigrant sentiment either, because the only real Americans are the Native Americans. You know what we did to them, right? People don't know about Juan Rodriguez. He was from Santo Domingo and came here aboard a Dutch ship in 1613. He married a Native American and traded with the Native Americans. He was here before the Pilgrims. That's why we It's a have a portion of Broadway called Juan Rodriguez Way. In the rest of America, we have the names Colorado, Arizona, Los Angeles,

San Antonio, La Florida. They didn't come from the sky. They came from somewhere.

"I will consider my career successful if some of the communities that I represent now stay here. If you stay, you're deeply rooted and have ownership. Inwood used to be all Irish. Also the Greeks, the Cubans, and the Jews were here, and they built their dreams, made money, did better, and left.

"It would be nice for the next generation to identify with this neighborhood. If my grandkids come back in the future and say, 'You know what? Let's go to the neighborhood where Grandpa was. Let's go have a good mofongo, a good mangú with queso frito.'

"If they come back and say, 'This is where it all began, this is the mother ship,' then I think I've done my job."

very diverse district of spunk.

1977

Rinto

Gabriel

PRVY A POSLEDNY SNEHOVY DEN
THE FIRST AND THE LAST SNOW

bRATISLAVE
IN bRATISLAVA

2

SLOVAKS
ETHNIC GROUP
NEW YORK CITY
7,018 TOTAL POPULATION (U.S. CENSUS ESTIMATE)

Artist Gabriel Levicky is a member of one
of New York City's smallest ethnic groups,
Slovaks, which make up less than 0.1 percent
of the city's population, but that doesn't
mean he doesn't have a big story to tell.

❝ I was born in Humenné in eastern Slovakia. It's where the movie *The Shop on Main Street* was set. It won an Oscar in 1965. It's about the Aryanization of Jewish property by Slovaks, meaning the forced transfer of Jewish businesses into Aryan hands. It's still one of the best films about the Holocaust.

"My parents were survivors. My mother was in Auschwitz-Birkenau, my father in Sachsenhausen, so they met after the war. They instantly fell in love, so to speak. What their concept of love was after this experience is very tricky to say. They never talked about the Holocaust experience.

"I was born in 1948 when the Communists took over Czechoslovakia. My father became a Communist. He and I were constantly clashing. The sixties were like a volcano, in terms of consciousness, arts, identity. I was a young poet, a hippie. I loved Allen Ginsburg and the beat generation. People were smuggling in records—Beatles, Stones, The Who. In 1968, the Soviets crushed the liberalization movement. And I, in my foolishness as a twenty-year-old immortal, stood in front of the Russian tanks. Luckily they didn't run me over.

"When you are young, the question of self-preservation—it's not coming into play. You just want to make your statement and stand behind it. Well, the Slovak secret service came after me. I used somebody else's passport and escaped to Israel. I identified myself as Jewish, but I wasn't clear what it meant. I was like, 'Here I am!' in my new identity as a Jew from Slovakia, but I had long hair, and people were spitting on me on the street.

"So I left and returned to Czechoslovakia after the Communist government declared amnesty to those who escaped. I was very vulnerable, so I went back. I signed Charter 77, a man-

ifesto demanding human rights, but after they published all the signatures, the cops came immediately. They interrogated me every day and put the pressure on me so much that I was really losing it. I finally said, 'OK, that's it. I'm not allowing these Communists to destroy me. I would rather die on the streets of New York as a homeless guy than give in.'

"I went through Hungary, Romania, Yugoslavia, Italia. The whole escape was a miracle. We were looked upon as dirty refugees from Eastern Europe, and that's why I associate so much with poor immigrants today. I escaped to the U.S. in 1979.

"I became a poet and a cartoonist and artist. I'm an executive member of the Czechoslovak Society for Arts & Sciences. I focus on films. I work with an organization in Slovakia called the National Memory Institute that collects evidence of Communist and Fascist impact on society. They inherited all the KGB documents. They found my file and 350 pages were missing. I found out—yes—that some people were spying on me, but I wasn't shocked, really. They failed miserably as human beings and as ethical beings. But I understand why. They were afraid. Everybody was.

"Freedom is an unstoppable trend. It's an avalanche. As we know in human history, there are always those who want change via democratic means and those who want to do it by force and oppression. After the Berlin Wall fell in 1989, the revolutionaries in Czechoslovakia were mostly intellectuals, actors, writers, painters.

"In 1993, the country split, and it became the Czech Republic and the Republic of Slovakia. But there is always a connection—an umbilical

Freedom is an unstoppable trend.

cord—between both countries. I consider myself Czecho-Slovak. Slovakia's a very small country—about 5 million people—so that explains why there are so few of us here in New York.

"I just ran into a group of young Slovaks—an art collective called Nástupište 1-12. The name means Gates 1-12. They were such ambitious, curious, talented people. They were young, they were vigorous, they had a vision, they had a direction, they had great art. And I was so pleased to see that. And I told myself, 'This is exactly what I was fighting for—for this freedom.' You don't have to escape. Instead, you travel, you gain experience, you bring it back, you utilize it, and you continue to endeavor and enrich both ways, you know?"

This is exactly what I was fighting for.

3

RAMBLERSVILLE
NEIGHBORHOOD
SOUTHWESTERN QUEENS

½ SQUARE MILE

Catherine M. Doxsey has spent most of her ninety-three years in Ramblersville, a nineteenth century fishing enclave turned twentieth century summer getaway turned today's smallest neighborhood in New York City. The great-grandmother has weathered all sorts of storms, including battling city hall for sewage lines, defending Ramblersville's reputation against detractors, and, most recently, fighting for her home after Hurricane Sandy decimated it.

❝ Gee whiz, I remember being very young. I couldn't get over the boardwalk. The sound of it was music to my ears. The salt air—my God! Those beautiful shells that you hold up to your ear and you hear the ocean pounding. Wow, what a place. It knocked my socks off.

"I was married April 12th, 1942. The war was on. He was twenty-one, and I was eighteen. He was the handsomest thing I ever saw. He knew it, though. He went to World War II straight away. By September I found out I was having a baby.

"I've lived in this house since 1954. It was on sale for seven thousand dollars, but my husband, Wilbur, screwed them down to six. I'm on the wetlands. We'd get a full moon and an east wind, and the tide would come in the house. I would drain it out, but I loved the place. We had an old rowboat. When the tide came in I rowed the kids over to 99th Street where the sidewalk wasn't underwater.

"The neighborhood is called Ramblersville because no two houses face the same way. People have rotten names for Ramblersville. They call it 'Down in The Hole.' The neighborhood's been neglected. It's been let go. It's always been looked down on. That's all right, because we're tougher than they are. I used to take my son into the yard and tell him, 'This is sacred soil in the United States of America.'

"Hurricane Sandy had a bad effect on me. I didn't want to leave. I took 49 inches in the house. If I had stayed I would have drowned. I left here with my dog and cat and a few medicines.

I thought I'd be back in two days. It was two years before I was back.

"All the furniture floated. Everything fell. The entire house had to be gutted—the floors, the walls, the electric, everything. It was a horror show. I came back because I love it here. I have to be by the water, I know that.

"The city tried to buy us out, but there's all kinds of regulations. I would have to buy another house in the city. I said, 'What? Do you think I'm out of my mind?' I'm not going to buy a place in the city. What for? A lot of people. A lot of cars. A lot of buses. It's so quiet here. The sky is so beautiful in Ramblersville. Blue, white, and clouds. You don't see that in the city. It's nothing but cement."

4

RAT ISLAND
PRIVATELY OWNED ISLAND
CITY ISLAND HARBOR, THE BRONX
2½ ACRES (LOW TIDE)/1 ACRE (HIGH TIDE)

They say it's called Rat Island because convicts
escaping from a nearby prison stopped there
in their swim to freedom. But, for the island's
owner, Alex Schibli, the tiny lump of bedrock
is his very own Atlantis in the Atlantic.

I left Switzerland to live here because of the water. They don't have big water over there in Switzerland. When I came to the States in 1967 I went sailing here, and that's how I discovered City Island.

"I live in a house on the water and can see Rat Island from my kitchen window when I am doing the dishes. I used to paddle out in the kayak and I got to know the owner. Boaters were stopping off and leaving behind beer bottles and stuff like that. So I said to him, 'Look. I'm cleaning up your island. I'm going to have to send you a bill.' And he said, 'Well, I'll have to charge you rent if you go to my island.'

A few years later, it went up for auction. The *Wall Street Journal* wrote that Ivanka Trump was looking to develop condos on it. Hundreds of people showed up at the auction.

"But by the second round there were only three of us left. It was a little bit tense. You have a certain number in your mind that you're not going to go over. But I did go over it. My girlfriend tried to stop me. She wasn't so happy. I paid $160,000. It's the only privately owned island in New York City.

"To have an island in the ocean for someone from a landlocked country—that's something very special. Now, my island has an American flag and a Swiss flag on it. We go out there for picnics. Sometimes I even swim out. It's only 500 meters from my backyard. The water's clean, like Orchard Beach.

"It's zoned for residential, but the only thing living out there is a blue heron. We had Canada Geese breeding there, but the seagulls don't like them. Then I have American oystercatchers that come.

Lots of people have boats,

"We worked with a famous Swiss artist to put a statue of William Tell on the island. William Tell was a Swiss liberation fighter from the 1300s. A foreign emperor tried to capture Switzerland, and William Tell refused to bow to him. The emperor said, 'You should go to prison. But I'll give you one chance. Shoot the apple off your son's head with your crossbow and I will set you free.'

"William Tell was an expert marksman, and he shot right through the middle of the apple. His son didn't even break a sweat.

"A lot of people—my kids included—thought I was crazy when I bought it. But I tell everyone, 'Lots of people have boats, but I have an island.'"

but I have an island.

5

WEST FOURTH STREET COURTS ("THE CAGE")

BASKETBALL COURT

GREENWICH VILLAGE, MANHATTAN

2,869 SQUARE FEET

All summer long, spectators crowd behind a chain-link fence to watch some of the best street ball there is. But because the concrete basketball court is half the size of a regulation court, the play there can get intense. Arnie Segarra, who played pick-up ball there as a kid and now serves as the court's "Honorary Commissioner," explains how it works inside "The Cage."

❝ There are a lot of challenges on such a tiny court. You have to run quicker. You have to shoot the shot quicker. It makes you a better player.

"It gets intense, and it gets physical. That kind of play is called 'banging inside.' Players are screaming and fighting. The testosterone is exploding. That's the law of the street in action you are watching.

Yet, somehow players still manage to slip in a quick, 'Hey, you're pretty' to the girls who are watching. The players play to the fans and the people walking by. It gets dramatic. The tourists like it.

"The rules of the game are the same as anywhere else, but they're not enforced. If I hit you and you didn't bleed, there was no foul. But, at the same time, the level of play is so high. You get the funky guys yelling and cursing. And then you get the structure and the play that is unrivaled on other street courts.

"You get players from the top colleges. You have guys here that play in Kentucky, North Carolina—but they're New York City kids. They come back for the summer and play. Dr. J, Walter Berry, Anthony Mason, and Smush Parker all played here. So the West Fourth Courts—it's everything. I would describe it as the finest street ball in the NBA. It combines the best of both those worlds.

"It all started back in the late sixties. NYU was one of the top basketball teams in the country. They'd take a study break to play, and people would come out and challenge them: Happy Hairston, who played with the Lakers; Tom 'Satch' Sanders, who played with the Celtics; Kyle Ramsey, who played with the Knicks.

"I was raised in the Johnson Houses of East Harlem and was in a street gang called the Viceroys. I went to college on a basketball scholarship and started playing down here in 1967. I've always been an activist and a community organizer. Now I'm on the New York City Commission on Human Rights.

"But here on the basketball court, I'm like an honorary commissioner. They dedicated a bench in my honor fifty years after I first came down here. The courts have always been a part of my life. I'm the one who helped to get the permits because sometimes there's been a little bit of racism down here, and the power people in the Village didn't want a league.

"But the truth is it was safer for kids to come down here and play basketball than some of the neighborhoods uptown. So to get away from where they lived, they'd come down to Greenwich Village. And, unbeknownst to them, they created this historical basketball court with an international name. But, yeah, to them, they just came out to play."

6

CATHEDRAL LIBRARY
LIBRARY
MIDTOWN, MANHATTAN
2,130 SQUARE FEET

Call it a book nook, a subterrestrial athenaeum, a commuter's lyceum, or a sunken treasure. New York's tiniest library, located below street level and inside a subway station, manages to be all of those things and a tiny bit more. Library manager Susan Aufrichtig explains why.

"We like to think of ourselves as fully functioning because we have everything the bigger libraries do, just on a smaller, cuter underground scale. Totally underground.

"We are a little hidden gem because everyone is delighted at finding us here, because nobody expects to come up out of the subway and see a library. We're often asked to help people with the MetroCard machines. They think we're actually connected to the subway. We also do a lot of directional stuff for tourists: 'Times Square is that way.'

"We are right off the E, M, and 6 lines at 51st Street, so we're built for the commuter's convenience—people running in and out of the subway to drop off books and pick up weekend reading. Because we're on a small scale, we know almost all of our patrons, so it's really personal. It's like a little family down here.

"Working underground is OK. We have no windows, so people come in, and they'll be wet, and we're like, 'Oh, is it raining outside?' It's like a casino that way.

"We're closed on the weekends because our entrance to the subway stop closes. There's a big, circular glass door upstairs that swings shut. It makes our little

we're offering

library even more intriguing. We have a book discussion group that runs until 6:45 p.m., and I'm like, 'Time to go! Because, otherwise, you'll get locked in the library.' Which is also an allure, because everybody wants to be in a library after it closes.

"When I started working in a library, I thought, 'This is what I want to do for the rest of my life.' There is no stereotypical librarian anymore because of the movie, *Party*

Girl. Parker Posey made librarian stuff cool. She was a rebellious party girl—like many librarians. It changed what a lot of people think of librarians. So thank you, Parker Posey.

"A lot of people don't think libraries even have a place in this world anymore, but we're needed more than ever. And then there's the whole 'fake news' thing. Librarians can help people navigate between fake news and authoritative news. So much of what is available through Google just scratches the surface, but the library has the resources to help you dig further.

"I've always loved reading. It takes you out of your own life and lets you travel the world without actually leaving the confines of your little tiny library. So, even though we're tiny and underground, we're offering the world to people here. And I think that's why I read—to travel widely, without actually traveling. Just traveling in your mind."

the world to people here.

7

Q TRAIN
DISTANCE BETWEEN STOPS
FLATBUSH, BROOKLYN
400 METERS

The Cortelyou and Beverley Road subway stops
on the Q line are just one block apart—the
closest two stations in New York City. Runner
Adam Devine always found it pointless that
they were so close together. So why not do
something equally as pointless? Try to outrun
the train by jumping out of a subway car and
sprinting to the next station in time to jump
back on the same train before it pulls out.

❝ I live on the Q line, and every time I'm on the train I'm like, 'Why do we have to stop here *and* there?' It doesn't make any sense. The train hasn't even fully left one station before it begins to enter the other one. Being a runner in New York City, my idea of how far things are is skewed. I'm like, 'Why wouldn't I just walk there?' Where other people are like, 'Why in the world would I walk there?'

"Racing this thing—I felt like I was being hunted. It was like the train was chasing me.

"Getting up the stairs was the hardest part. At the turnstile, I was just focused on swiping the card. I flubbed and had to re-swipe. When I came jetting out, everybody coming in was like, 'What the hell's going on?' It's hard for people to notice craziness in New York, but they acknowledged something unordinary was going on, which was nice.

"I heard the brakes as it pulled into the station, and I was sure I wasn't going to make it. But when I got halfway down the staircase I realized, 'Oh, my God, the train's still here!' And then I was like, 'Wait. Are the doors still open?' They weren't.

"It took me 81 seconds, and the train takes 67 seconds. To actually beat it, I would have to knock 14 seconds off—so almost

It's hard for people to notice craziness in New York

a minute per mile faster. Usain Bolt could do it. It wouldn't be a problem for him, but he'd have to work a little bit.

"In 2008, I got run over by a hit-and-run drunk driver and ended up gaining a lot of weight after the accident. I decided to start walking to get healthy again. That turned into running, and I signed up for the Brooklyn Half Marathon. It was torture. I saw these Prospect Park Track Club members run by. They had cheer squads along the course, and I was thinking, 'I'm not having fun. They're having fun. I want to hang out with those people and have fun.'

"Now I'm team captain. Running is usually a solitary act. When you're running by yourself, it's easy to think, 'I can't do this.'

"In New York, you run into a lot of people, and on the subway you're packed up against a lot of people, but you don't interact with them. It's so easy to feel alone, even in a city of 14 million people. But now it's almost impossible for me to feel alone when I'm running."

8

PUMPS EXOTIC DANCING
STRIP CLUB
EAST WILLIAMSBURG, BROOKLYN

1,200 SQUARE FEET

When Andy Sig opened Pumps Bar in 1997,
Mayor Rudolph Giuliani was intent on driving
the adult entertainment industry out of business,
and Williamsburg had nary a hipster in sight.
Two decades later, a lot has changed—
except for Pumps, which has remained
true to its founding mission.

" We were the first club to open up under Giuliani's new 60/40 law. The city was pushing strip clubs and porn shops out of Times Square and residential areas. Before I opened up, I had to go to a town hall meeting. There were 300 people there. Senators, congressmen, newspapers—it was out of control. And I had to stand there while everyone ripped me to pieces.

"One guy got up and said, 'Look at these people ruining our beautiful neighborhood.' And I'm thinking, 'You've got to be kidding me. There's hookers and pimps everywhere. It was the worst people in the world here. And to tell you the truth, that's why I hired the worst people in the world: to combat the worst people in the world. It was like the Old West. We'd throw anyone who was acting up out the swinging doors.

"About eight years ago the area started getting really hipstery. The clientele went from leather jackets and biker apparel to musicians

and artists without calluses on their hands. You know how else I knew the area was really changing? ATM usage was way up. Our original patrons didn't go to the ATM. They had cash. They were drug dealers and gangsters.

"I wasn't worried gentrification was going to hurt our business. Why? Because everybody likes tits.

"Back then, the girls were also a lot different. They were always going to be dancers unless they found a husband. Whereas, now, every girl is working here as a stepping-stone. This is

They all have dreams and aspirations to be something.

"This is not a normal strip club. This is an old school titty bar. This is not a gentleman's club. Because it's so small, the stage is behind the bar. That's the best way to make money because you can't avoid the bar.

"My parents were totally behind me opening the bar. My mother comes here. My father comes here. My aunts come here. Sometime I bring my kids down here on a Sunday when we're closed, and they go crazy on the poles.

"People have fallen in love here. Plenty of people. First of all, I married my wife, who was a dancer here. How's that for starters? Now she tends bar every weekend. She is the energy of this club. When my wife works, she makes everyone happy.

"I would say my wife and I are all about not judging people. It's all

not a normal strip club.

out on the table. We wear our hearts on our sleeve, and we're very open people. That's it. There's nothing hidden."

9

AJ YELLOW TAXI TUTORS
CABBIE SCHOOL
JACKSON HEIGHTS, QUEENS
560 SQUARE FEET

If you've ever ridden in a yellow taxi with a South Asian cabbie, odds are it was AJ Gogia—the Taxi Guru—who schooled the driver on how to ace the taxi test. So it's not for nothing that Gogia's basement classroom under the elevated Number 7 train is referred to as the 'Stanley Kaplan of Taxi School.'

" I came to America from India when I was eighteen. I started driving a cab in college while all my friends were working at The Gap for five dollars an hour. I would work one day and make more than they made in a month.

"The job was just fantastic. It's amazing how the city comes alive at night. One time a person entered my cab dressed like a man and came out dressed like a woman. It was like, 'I remember picking up a man, and did I just drop a woman?'

"When I was still in college I got a job teaching taxi school. I did it for a few years, and then came the Wall Street boom. All of my friends were making boatloads of money in finance.

"I was making good money but not Wall Street money, so I quit my job and became a financial advisor. I was making lots of *moolah*, but there was no satisfaction. There was excessive use of alcohol and drugs, which I don't do. I said to myself, 'I can't do this. This is no good for you.' And I just left.

"In 2004, I opened my own school. I teach them to pass the exam on New York City geography and Taxi & Limousine Commission rules and regulations. The test is two hours and eighty questions. The pass/fail rate is fifty percent. But, for my students, the pass rate is 90 percent.

"My Wall Street friends are super smart guys. They would sit in my

class for fun and be lost. A question could be, 'You pick up a customer from Prospect Park, and he wants to go to FiDi. How will you go there?' My friends had no idea.

"My teaching style works because I make it entertaining. It's a stand-up routine, but I'm also on top of them. I'm like the mean guy who runs the boarding school dorm. I make them laugh when I'm berating one of their classmates. I'm an equal opportunity berater.

I sleep so peacefully at night.

"My students are from India, Pakistan, Bangladesh, Nepal, Tibet, Myanmar, West Africa—Guinea, Ivory Coast, Senegal, Mali, and North Africa—Morocco, Algeria, Egypt. We get every now and then a few Yemenites, but not a lot.

"We run a very holy atmosphere here. It's very personal. I make it a point to remember everybody's name.

"They choose to become taxi drivers for a few reasons. It's flexible. They can go home for six months. What kind of a job lets you go home for six months? Then there's the money. They could be making two grand in cash a week—after expenses—if they know what they're doing. Like, you can't be cruising on York Avenue at three in the morning. You need to be where the action is. Everybody's not that smart. You have to know the streets. You have to know the city.

"But the main reason they want to drive a taxi is that it's a 'halal' way to make a living. A lot of guys are Muslims and don't want to work in a store selling cigarettes and alcohol. At a bodega, they'd be enablers. Driving a cab, they get to stand with their values and still make a living.

"I sleep so peacefully at night. I sleep like a baby. People are happy. I'm helping them make a living. When Indians pass the test, they come touch my feet, even if they're older than me. It's a sign of respect. And they all bring in Indian sweets when they pass. Sometimes we'll have fifteen boxes of sweets a day in here. I tell people to take them home. I can't eat any more sweets. My teeth hurt."

I sleep like a baby.

10

SUTTON CLOCK SHOP
CLOCK REPAIR
YORKVILLE, MANHATTAN
660 SQUARE FEET

The Sutton Clock Shop is not a place where
time stands still. It's a place for clocks that
have come to a standstill. And Sebastian
Laws, horologist and son of a horologist,
never fails to get time moving again.

" People come in with stories like, 'My grandfather's father gave him this clock.' There's this whole lineage of people and their clocks. People love their clocks.

"A clock is always in the background. People are always looking at it but not really perceiving it. They only notice it when it stops working.

"The sound is a big part, too. You don't notice it chiming, but you

notice when it stops. There are all these sort of subliminal connections that people have with their clocks.

"We have clocks here that are 200 years old and they still work. These clocks are brass and metal. It breaks, you take another piece of brass, solder it on, file it down, and you make another gear. You can keep making that same clock work so 200 years from now it's still working. You can't imagine anything digital working after even five years. It just stops and that's it.

"Horologists used to scribe their name and date inside the clock. Sometimes you open a clock and see a name and imagine that guy in England in the 1800s. Could he imagine 150 years later it would be somewhere in New York being fixed? I etch my name into it, so I can wonder 150 years from now where that clock will be with both our names on it.

"I didn't know I was going to follow in my father's footsteps and take over the business. I was a singer in a rock/hip-hop

Just enjoy time

band and then started working more in the shop. When he passed away I took over.

"All us clock guys are a little different, but one thing you have to be is patient. It can take hours to figure out what the problem is because you are working with such small pieces. One piece less than one millimeter off can make the entire clock stop, so you have to be calm. I don't fly off the handle easily.

"I'm a pretty prompt person, but I'm not obsessed with time. I try to enjoy every moment. People say, 'Oh, I don't like to waste time because you can't get it back.' You're not doing anything, you're not doing anything. Don't always try to do something. Just enjoy time as it is.

"I love going all over the five boroughs to fix clocks because everybody's got clocks. You go from the swankiest apartment on Park Avenue all the way out to Brownsville, and you see everybody with their clocks and their clocks interacting in their houses. It's like a back road to New York's secrets."

as it is.

11

THE LITTLE VICTORY THEATRE
COMMUNITY PLAYHOUSE
TRAVIS, STATEN ISLAND
496 SQUARE FEET (FORTY-EIGHT SEATS)

Before retired cop Alberta Thompson founded the tiniest community theater on Staten Island, her experience in the dramatic arts was limited to going undercover to buy drugs, entertaining spectators while working crowd control at the New York City Marathon, and starring in police training videos.

The Department was doing training films showing recruits how not to behave on an interview. So I got filmed chewing the gum and doing the real New York accent thing and saying, 'So. Like. Just wondering. How long is this going to take? I'm just curious because I gotta go for a manicure.'

"I grew up on Staten Island. I went for a Katharine Gibbs school degree and learned stenography. I was a secretary on Wall Street, and I had a boyfriend who was a cop. I thought it was the most wonderful thing to do—to help people, to have an exciting life, to change the world.

"I came on in 1983. The NYPD had just dropped the height requirement. I'm only five feet tall. I worked on the Lower East Side, and it was serious drugs—a lot of violence. Everybody had a gun in those days. I met my husband on a sting operation. His job was to buy cocaine, so he was rolling around on the floor pretending he needed drugs. We fell in love that day.

"My big thing has always been comedy. I love to make people laugh. As a cop, I would work a parade or marathon and get a circle of people around me. It was like entertainment. I loved it. I retired in 2002.

"Fast forward to 2013. I saw a little tiny ad. A local theater company was doing auditions for *Death of A Salesman*. I went in and had this killer audition out of nowhere. It was for Linda Loman, the lead. I had never really acted before. It was the most coveted role on Staten Island by the veteran actresses. They were like, 'Who are you? Where'd you come from?' They couldn't have been more horrible to me.

I had faced guns and felt less terror.

"Opening night was terrifying. I had faced guns and felt less terror. But somehow, when you come out onto that stage, it just disappears. Especially when you have the audience with you.

"This is my philosophy: I built this little theater to harken back to when the world was a kinder, simple place. It was built to be safe and a happy place. I don't do slit-your-wrists theater in here. Sometimes people come in with a heavy heart, and they leave like somebody's just given them a breath of fresh air.

"We started with forty-eight seats, but we can squeeze in sixty-two, and I'm talking cheek-to-cheek. Squished.

"One actor came in and said, 'This place is really small.' And I said, 'Right. So what part of The…Little…Victory…Theatre didn't you get? Just out of curiosity. What part did you not get? Did you not get the 'The' or the 'Little'?"

12

LITTLE PICASSO CHILDREN'S ART STUDIO
KIDDIE ART SCHOOL
UPPER EAST SIDE, MANHATTAN
480 SQUARE FEET

Isabella Grossman is a former Israeli soldier, the holder of a fine arts degree from Fashion Institute of Technology, and a grandmother. And she runs her tiny art studio for children accordingly—with equal parts toughness, imagination, and love.

" I was raised in Israel in the countryside outside Haifa. I used to love walking into the woods to explore nature. I would come home and draw the flowers I picked or the mountains behind our house. My mother, when she realized my passion, gave me a wall that was my very own wall to draw on.

"She was a Holocaust survivor. She kept her sanity in the camps with art. She made things out of mud—sculpting out of the dirt and mud in the camps. She was an artist, but she never had the privilege of being trained and schooled.

We are

"We are all born artists. We all have that inherent primordial need to express ourselves. For most kids, as soon as they are standing up and grabbing things, the first thing they do when they have a crayon is go to a wall and start drawing on it. I named this studio after Picasso because he himself said, 'Every child is an artist. The problem is how to remain an artist when we grow up.'

"We get contaminated by life. A child's mind is pure and clean and unhindered by any complications of the adult world. Their absorption is pure. What they hear, what they see, what they touch, everything is pure.

"My granddaughter is the reason I opened this studio. I had a successful career as a fashion designer in China. Then my daughter got pregnant, and I had a dilemma. Should I stay in Guangzhou? Or take a risk and come back

to the U.S. and be part of my grandchild's life? I came back, and my worst fears came true. I couldn't find a job. So I spent a lot of time with my granddaughter. And, as soon she was old enough to grab things, I started teaching her art. I realized I was creating a little Picas-ette.

"When I actually opened the studio and parents started seeing what the kids were coming home with, they didn't believe their kids were actually doing it themselves. The rule is two- to four-year-olds have to be accompanied by a parent

all born artists.

or caregiver. I don't allow nannies or parents to sit here with their phones in their hands. Sometimes they get insulted. They get hurt, and those that don't understand? Goodbye. Thank you. The kids' attention spans are so short, anything will disrupt the flow of energy.

"One of the students, a three-year-old, insisted on having her doll and the other kids were watching her instead of working on their projects. So I asked the nanny to ask her to let the little doll rest and then when she goes home she can have it back. Well, the child started picking up chairs and throwing them at her nanny so I asked the nanny to take her home. The mom got very upset. She said, 'Well, I gave her permission to have the doll,' but I said, 'Well this is my domain. At home you do as you please. Here, I make the

rules. Because I'm not in the business of babysitting. I'm in the business of teaching art.

"First, I teach them how to recognize basic shapes in everything they see. Then I show them how to put those shapes together in a configuration that resembles the object we're drawing. I even teach them perspective. I make up songs about primary colors and how to hold a paintbrush because their first instinct is to take the brush and shmush it and destroy it. I go through a lot of brushes.

"It's practice, practice, practice. It doesn't happen overnight. I take them as young as two years old. If they last here, by the time they are five years old, they are artists. Every one of them."

13

STUDIO LOFT
CO-OP APARTMENT
FINANCIAL DISTRICT, MANHATTAN
400 SQUARE FEET

Marriage means not just merging the lives of two
people but combining their stuff—a challenge
for any couple—especially when the couple
resides in a tiny studio apartment. But it becomes
ridiculously challenging when a baby comes
along. Jill Slater explains how her family of three
manages in an apartment without a bedroom.

" "It's technically 400 square feet but if you count the loft it's 640 square feet. If you're under 5 foot 6, you think this is a two-floor apartment. If you're over 5 foot 6, you think, 'Oh, what a nice storage area upstairs to crawl around in.' My husband is 5 foot 10, and he doesn't think we have a two-floor apartment. My daughter is three and thinks we have this huge house.

"When Marc and I got married, I had this place, and he had a one-bedroom on the Upper East Side, and I wanted nothing to do with the Upper East Side. Our lives were so different it was hard to merge them, so we co-existed in many ways—real estate included. We went back and forth between our apartments. It's seven miles. I bike everywhere, and I was a giant pack mule. I could be carrying a sewing machine, a child, and vegetables.

"It wasn't until last year, at the behest of Marc's ninety-one-year-old Uncle Godfrey, who said, 'You've got to start living in the same place, because it'll save you money.'

"The main sacrifice was getting rid of a lot, Marc doesn't like clutter, and there are clothes that I cannot get rid of. Am I going to give away my Fiorucci fur-lined vest from 1986? No!

"Marc's big request was to be able to rotate 365 degrees while getting dressed and not

hit anything with his elbow, so I re-did the closet and widened the doorway.

"The floor space in the kitchen is 6 square feet. You learn how to choreograph so you don't get hit in the head by the refrigerator or block the oven door. When Marc and I are in there together, he always says, 'This is a one-man job.' So I have to leave.

"I had built a stage area at one end of the apartment to put storage underneath it. We put Slater's crib up there

temporarily and spent a lot of time thinking about where she would go. While we were deliberating, she somehow figured out how to sleep with light and noise pollution. The challenge is that babysitters sit here in the dark, and I tiptoe around her at night. We'll figure it out before Slater gets to high school.

"The fact is that when you have a child, you realize they know what you give them to know. Whatever rituals you set up, whatever norms you establish, they think that's normal. And a lot of times that's good and then there's the flip side—terrible situations where they don't know anything else and therefore they think that is how people live."

14

MAYSLES CINEMA
MOVIE THEATER
HARLEM, MANHATTAN
350 SQUARE FEET (FIFTY-FIVE SEATS)

Five-year-old Samad Ibn-Kahlil Bell took in a recent screening of *I Am Not Your Negro* at the snug Maysles Cinema in Harlem, the first theater in New York City dedicated exclusively to documentaries. Samad's father, Kahlil Kwame Bell, explained why he brought his pre-K-aged son to see a film that's been called an "advanced seminar on racial politics in America."

My friend had tickets, and the minute he told me the film was dealing with James Baldwin I said, 'I will bring Samad.'

"James Baldwin is one of America's top writers, and not just because he writes so eloquently about topics of race and class, but because he writes about just wanting fairness. He was not asking for anything more than fairness. It's very important for kids to know about him and the movement he was a part of because kids now are not taught to acknowledge the past.

"I brought Samad because I want him to see someone who looks like him fight for what's right. I want him to see a black man stand up for justice and speak articulately about various facets of injustices and social ills, that, when addressed properly and firmly, can incite change. Most importantly, I want him to see the time period of his grandmother, what she lived through and the things she saw.

"We saw the Malcolm X movie with Denzel Washington, and when he saw the real Malcolm X in this documentary he knew exactly who he was immediately. He can identify Malcolm X more quickly than Martin Luther King, which is extremely rare for a child his age.

"Normally, when kids are being taught about the Civil Rights Movement, it's only about MLK. After a while, if you're not a Christian, it seems uneven. The only fundamental difference between Dr. King and Malcolm X is that Malcolm X believed you should defend yourself. Other than that, there was not much difference between them.

kids now are not taught to acknowledge the past.

"Dr. King wasn't saying, 'Jesus, Jesus, Jesus,' and Malcolm X wasn't saying, 'Allah, Allah, Allah,' all the time.

"I own the movies *Roots*, *Glory*, *Malcolm X*, and *Blade*. *Blade* is because Samad is studying the martial arts, and there are no black martial arts movies except for *Blade*, really. I allow him to see those movies because they are historically relevant to his existence. So that when he is experiencing a blessing, he can always connect it to someone in the past who fought for that blessing—whether it's sitting in the front of the bus or getting hired for a certain job or being able to make an amount of money that would have been unthinkable a few generations ago.

"We are taught in this country to be submissive to a white supremacy regime, and, because we are taught to do that, we pick and choose our battles. That's another thing he has to learn: As a man, if you are gonna die, it can't be for something foolish, like your wallet.

"When I was eight, my mom took me to go see *For Colored Girls Who Have Considered Suicide*. I remember not really understanding it, but I knew I was witnessing black artistry at a high level. When children see such high artistry in music, theater, documentaries, it allows them to imagine themselves in that time and to make a connection to how it's relevant to them now.

"The best time to start is before they're teenagers looking for social acceptance. If you expose them to a lot of things early on, when they are faced with confrontation they will always have a point of reference to know there is something better someplace else. A lot of times, kids only know their house, the store down the block, their car—so it's important to take them out of their comfort zone.

"I think what Samad will gather from this movie is he saw someone fighting for something and then, later on, he will realize how important that is to his life now. He'll always be able to say, 'My dad showed me a documentary about that when I was young.'"

15

A&A BAKE & DOUBLES SHOP
TRINIDADIAN STREET FOOD
BEDFORD-STUYVESANT, BROOKLYN
350 SQUARE FEET

This husband-and-wife-run place sells doubles—
Trinidad and Tobago's most popular street food.
Customers line up early and around the block
for the messy but perfect-tasting sandwich,
which is made of fried flat bread, curried
chickpeas, and tropical chutneys. Noel Brown
and his wife Geeta ship in fresh ingredients from
Trinidad, and customers can even pay in T&T
Dollars, the currency of their home island.

In Trinidad, we have breakfast, basically, all day. They all go for doubles for breakfast. It's the perfect hangover meal, too. It's like a cure. It works because it's very spicy. The spices wake you up quick. They consume all the alcohol inside you.

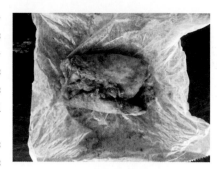

"One double is a buck fifty. Doubles is just two pieces of bread with chickpeas and chutney on top. The bread is deep-fried, and it's called *bara*. It's very thin, not too big; it's only two bites. Some people eat two, some eat three, some eat four. It all depends on how you feel that day or maybe how much you drank the night before.

"You put the spices and different ingredients to make the chickpea curry *channa*. Then there's the chutney. It's like a hot dog. There's the frank and the bun; then you add your ketchup and your mustard and your sauerkraut. Well, doubles is like that: At the end, you add the chutney. You have your hot and spicy sauce, you have the mild sauce, you have the in-between mild and hot sauce.

"Just like Trinidad is a blend of people and their cultures—African, British, Creole, French, Indian, and Spanish—doubles are a mix of flavors from all the different places. The curry originally came from India, but we took it and reinvented it in the Trinidad style.

"Most of our customers are Tobagonians and Trinidadians and some Grenadians. We get the cab drivers who wait in their cars at the start of their shifts and also the people from the islands

The spices wake you

who live around here. That's why we have a sign up saying we accept T&T Dollars. And we have our poster of Nicki Minaj because she was born in Trinidad. But she hasn't come in here yet.

"But the customers are not just Trinidadians. My business has increased with the gentrification because the people moving into the neighborhood are mostly vegetarian or vegan, and our stuff is vegetarian.

"When they first come, I really have to explain the taste to them and what it is, and then I ask them whether they want spicy or not spicy or in-between

up quick.

"They come back because it's fresh. You get it hot, and it's tasty. And because of the price. Two doubles and a drink—you get full here."

16

RESPECT FOR LIFE
BOOKS-N-THINGS
BLACK LIBERATION BOOKSTORE
BEDFORD-STUYVESANT, BROOKLYN
250 SQUARE FEET

Jibriel Muhammad has always questioned everything—religion, government, economic systems, cultural norms. He finally found the answers he was looking for in the Nation of Islam. So it makes sense Muhammad now owns a black liberation bookstore where people with questions might find the answers they are looking for.

" I grew up as a Catholic in Bedford-Stuyvesant. I went to church faithfully until I started to think for myself and ask rational questions. One day, I asked how Mary had a child with no physical father. The answer didn't make sense to me.

From there was my rite to passage into the street. I had no faith whatsoever until I was in my late twenties. I wanted to get serious and have a family, and spirituality was a part of that. I wanted a place that accepted all three books: Old Testament, New Testament, Koran. That was Islam. I started as an orthodox Muslim, but the culture was so drastically different with the dress and the sandals and the kufi and the beard. I wanted to remain who I am.

"Then I heard the Honorable Minister Louis Farrakhan speak and he sounded very balanced and rational. There used to be a store with a TV in the window that played his speeches. I would get a chair, sit in front of the window, and listen for hours.

"I picked it all apart, and everything was real. I knew this was where I needed to be.

"It was a big culture change. It gave me discipline. On the street, you're drinking, you're smoking, you're hanging out, you're partying, you're talking to girls, you're doing your thing. But inside a structured place like the Nation, the relationship is more on the spiritual level. You're bonding around something you all benefit from. It's not degrading or harmful to yourself.

"I am in the Nation of Islam, but this is not a Nation of Islam bookstore. This is a black liberation bookstore, meaning we try to bring consciousness to black people. To raise their vibration and their knowledge of history, spirituality, economics, health, relationships, family, masonry— whatever they might be looking for.

"For people who think the Nation hates white people, I would say we hate the mind of white supremacy. That is our worst enemy. That's the force that's killing black youth, that's racially profiling, that's gentrifying. Coming out of that, there's a lot of work we have to do internally.

"I think black people . . . we're trying to find our way. We know something needs to be done—I think we can all agree on that. But there are so many different mindsets in black America about what to do. The Nation

But they should always ask questions. Always.

of Islam perspective is that we need to do for self. Cover your home base first. Take care of your family, and create self-reliant communities.

"Our number one bestseller is *Message to the Blackman in America*, by the Honorable Elijah Muhammad. If they get through this, they're gonna have questions. Some people follow blindly because they like the discipline or the women or the dress or whatever. But they should always ask questions. Always."

17

HOUSE OF OLDIES
RECORD SHOP
WEST VILLAGE, MANHATTAN
345 SQUARE FEET

Twenty years ago, Bob Abramson put up a big sign in his window that said "No CDs, No Tapes, Just Records" because he didn't want to be bothered with all the idiots coming in asking for CDs and tapes. That subpar technology has come and gone, of course, while the sign—and the vinyl—remain.

" I'm proud of my bargain bin. Every record store has a bargain bin with what we call 'yard sale quality.' I would throw those in the garbage. There is not a store in the U.S. that has a bargain bin where every freaking record is perfect. Listen, I'm not gonna sell Justin Timberlake scratched up records. You understand? The first time he came in here, he walks over, shakes my hand, and says, 'My name's Justin.' And I says, 'I know who you are!' What a sweetheart. He buys Fleetwood Mac-type stuff. But I treat these people like anyone. I'm not starstruck.

"We have a reputation of being a little expensive and having top-quality stuff, which is the way I want to keep it.

"I grew up in Brooklyn, and my parents were poor. They didn't have a TV set, so when I was five I would lie in bed with a little Bakelite radio listening to Top 40 songs. I used my allowance to buy 45s.

"I love what I've done since 1968. I love the records. I love feeling the records. I love touching them. I love looking at

them. I love selling them. I love discussing them with the young people who come in.

"I'm not the original owner. I was a customer in the early sixties, and the business was going downhill, so the owner wanted to sell it to me. I realized he had the customers, but he didn't have the records. Somebody would ask for a Frankie Avalon single, and he would have ten singles but not 'Bobby Sox to Stockings' or 'Blue Jeans' or 'Venus.' None of the big hits. So I made a deal and took over the store.

"I would travel around the country in a station wagon. At that time, supermarkets sold 45's for a dime apiece. I would buy thousands at a time. If it was all Perry Como and Bing Crosby, I'd move on. If it was R&B and Shorty Lee and Big Joe Turner, I'd take the whole thing.

"People come in, and they can't believe it. That's one of the reasons I stay, because people actually love the store. They come in and go, 'I've arrived!' That's because it looks like a store from the 1960s, because it *is* a record store from the sixties I haven't changed anything!

"I've got about one hundred thousand records. It's kinda mixed up. See the Moody Blues? I had no room in the 'M' area because it was jammed up. So I just put them over there with Stevie Wonder where I had space. It's the 'I-don't-give-a-shit-look-for-yourself-system.'"

18

LHASA FAST FOOD
TIBETAN TAKEOUT
JACKSON HEIGHTS, QUEENS
240 SQUARE FEET

You don't need a sherpa to find the Lhasa Tibetan
restaurant. Just keep the money transfer store
to your left and the cell phone store on the
right. At the end of a narrow corridor, past the
Indian jewelry shop, you'll find chef Sang Jien
Ben cooking up the most miraculous momos
in town. (Note: If you hit the Little Myanmar
Mini Mart, you've wandered off course.)

" In Tibet, I was a monk. I joined the monastery at fifteen. We chanted. We studied. We were fed. We didn't have to worry about life.

"Then a friend invited me to come to America to visit. I found a lot of Tibetans here and a lot of religious freedom, so I stayed. But then I found that not everything was as I expected. I needed to work. That's when I decided to become a 'civilian.'

"At first, I worked in a Chinese restaurant. Every day, my work was to peel off the skin of the chicken and, every day, I needed to fry all the chicken thighs. In Tibet, we eat beef or lamb or yak. We usually eat one cow or one

sheep or one ox. A lot of people will share it. I had never eaten chicken before. It was just too much chicken. It was disgusting.

I found a lot of freedom, so I stayed.

"When I first opened the restaurant, I didn't have that much money. It was just a counter in the back of a cell phone store. I didn't even have a sign. I kept expanding it. I have two small children now, and I hope that I will have a real big-size restaurant someday, but I haven't found the place yet.

"My joy now is to cook and to present people with clean, healthy food. There's no way I can live a life here like I lived before. Now, all I desire is that people are happy eating the food that we provide. I just hope people will say, 'Wow, it's delicious, and the price is reasonable.'

"Ever since I was in the temple—ever since I was little—we were taught that peace is important. Usually we say, 'Peace to everybody.' That's what we value.

"I think it's very good that people in America are meditating. Now my meditation practice is that, when customers arrive, they eat the food, they are happy, so I'm happy. There's not much else I can do anymore."

19

FIRST PROFESSIONAL CLEANERS
DRY CLEANER
UPPER EAST SIDE, MANHATTAN
230 SQUARE FEET

How does a place that cleans your interview suit for free if you are unemployed manage to stay in business? Might be because it operates out of a speck of a space. Or because it's the best in the neighborhood. Or could be because of karma. Spend some time with owner Carlos Vasquez, and you'll probably decide it's all three.

" I grew up in Alphabet City. I told my mom we needed to move. I have three younger brothers, and I said, 'They're not gonna make it. Let's get out of here.' It was really tough. I got married early. I was seventeen.

"Out of high school, I got a job at a dry cleaner as a helper. The owner saw my dedication, so he sent me to cleaning school to learn how to press and take out spots. It's just you, a radio and a machine—bang, bang, bang. I'm more of a people person. I told my boss it wasn't for me. So he made me assistant manager.

"I actually went back to school to get out of this field. I graduated with an associate's in accounting and a 3.85 GPA. They gave me a scholarship to Fordham, but I couldn't go because I had a family to support.

"It's a competitive business. I charge a little more, but I am quality. With me, you don't get a missing button; my whites stay very white. I use two dry cleaning services just to keep them honest. I don't have

many do-overs come in here. If I have ten a year, that'll be too much.

"The store is tiny. But it's in and out. I pick it up. I get it done and 'Voom!' out of the store. When the delivery trucks come, it can get overwhelming, but me and my nephew and my wife, we know how to handle it.

"When the Twin Towers blew up in 2001, a lot of people from our zip code vanished. So many people were looking for jobs after that, so I put a sign up saying if you needed your suit cleaned for a job interview, I'd do it for free, and that policy stands to this day.

"We were worried because the costs come out of pocket. But it's a way to give back to my community,

and karma has a way of going around in circles. I was brought up that way. I'm a giver. It's from my mama—special woman. She raised seven of us, then went and raised six orphans.

"I don't want to be rich. I just want to be comfortable. I never wanted more stores, because I can't control what goes on there. Where we grew up, we learned not to trust anybody but family. I got my wife, I got my kids. At the end of the day, I'm a family man."

20

RIVINGTON GUITARS UNPLUGGED
ACOUSTIC GUITARS
EAST VILLAGE, MANHATTAN

224 SQUARE FEET

Stepping inside the shop that calls itself "NYC's Best Little Acoustic Guitar Store" is like walking into a giant guitar. The 8-foot-wide showroom is shaped like a fretboard and has wooden floors and walls, which are lined top-to-bottom with vintage Gibson Les Pauls, Telecasters, Stratocasters, and Jaguars. Owner Howie Statland's personal favorite is the 1952 Martin 00-18. To hear him describe its delights is like listening to a master sommelier discussing a fine vintage wine.

The "00" is the perfect-size guitar. It's not dreadnought-size; it's auditorium-size—a little bit smaller than the typical acoustic guitar. Pete Townshend used one to record *Tommy*. It's the playability and the sound. It sounds less boomy. It's got a sweet mid-range. It's cleaner, not too much muddiness on the bottom. It's like the Mediterranean Sea compared to the Hudson River.

"My mom's a concert pianist. She had me taking piano lessons very early. I was a pretty bad boy, though. At thirteen, I discovered The Who and Pete Townshend smashing his guitars. That's what I really wanted to do. I liked the aggressiveness of jumping around, smashing stuff.

"I am infatuated with guitars. Anytime I saw somebody playing one, I wanted to know what kind of guitar it was and how it worked and everything about it. When I'm done with work, all I want to do is talk about guitars. My wife is like, 'How do you do it?'

"We don't sell any new guitars. I like stuff that's a little worn. Before 1964, when The Beatles hit, they made the best guitars. After that, the quality went down because they had to make so many. The old stuff is hard to find.

"My buying coup was when I found out about a guy who had a perfect Gibson 1959 ES-335TD. It had been his dad's and he needed to sell it to buy a house because he just had a kid. I met him in a kitchen of an Elks Lodge in Upstate New York with a pile of cash. When these things come up, you'll drive to the end of the earth to get one.

"Robert Plant came in here once. That was pretty cool. No, it was really cool. He spent a couple of hours talking about the old days of Zeppelin. He was checking out this Fender 12-string electric, which 'Stairway to Heaven' was recorded on. So I plugged it in, and played the solo for 'Stairway to Heaven,' and he pulls the plug out. And he goes, 'STAIRWAY DENIED!' It was so trippy.

"Most of our customers are older, but we get young kids in here wanting to play. The guitar is such a hallmark of America, and it's so ingrained in American culture. You're always going to have teenagers with angst who want to grab a guitar and rock it out. You can't do that on a keyboard. Guitars are cooler. I think rock and roll will never die."

21

SURAN'S YOGA SPACE
YOGA STUDIO
JACKSON HEIGHTS, QUEENS

210 SQUARE FEET

Suran Song runs a yoga studio out of a one-
room studio apartment, which also quintuples
as her art studio, her office, her husband's
workspace, and their home. In order to turn
their wee apartment into a place with space
for all those endeavors, they did the most Zen
thing ever—got rid of all their furniture.

"I was teaching yoga at a Laundromat through The Laundromat Project, a nonprofit that uses art and culture to transform laundromats into rich spaces for communities of color. People did yoga while waiting for their wash. It was great fun. Some ladies had just come from Tibet. Some were from Mexico, a lot from Colombia.

"It was so small, I would teach in the doorway. Once it got cold I couldn't keep it up, and my husband said, 'Why don't we empty out all of our furniture and turn the apartment into a yoga space?' And I was like, 'Really?' Give up the couch and the TV and the bookshelves and the dining table and the bed? What are you? Crazy?'

"My husband and I met playing punk rock. He's got this great kind of Protestant work ethic, like, 'You don't need a chair, you should be doing something.' Now we live on tatami mats. We basically live and sleep and eat and work on the floor.

"It has its challenges. Instead of carving out space, what we really have to carve out is time. On certain days, I'll be at home working on art stuff, and my husband will be working on coding stuff. But, most of the time, we leapfrog so that he goes to work at a library or I go to a museum to draw.

"I don't do the Facebook or any social media. I'm kind of a Luddite. Then one day Google called. A lady with an Indian accent said, 'Do you do yoga there?' I'm like, 'Yes.' She's like, 'Is it a yoga studio?' I'm like, 'Well, kind of. It's where I live.' And she's like, 'OK.'

"Then it was on the map. I don't know how they know what's going on. It was a little like Big Brother.

"I came to New York to study sculpture and performance art. I started to think about how I could make a social sculpture using yoga in the same way a painter would use a canvas and a brush—using yoga to make a peaceful space together, a sort of dustless world or a garden, a meditative space where people could come together and be neighbors instead of passersby crammed on the subway or competing in an economy.

"I think art will save the world. It's a universal language that brings appreciation of each other—not just tolerance—but real respect.

"Queens is the most ethnically diverse urban area in the entire world. It *is* the whole world. It's ten years I've been living here, and every day I still just think, 'Yay!'"

22

THNK1994 MUSEUM
FEMINIST MICROMUSEUM
BEDFORD-STUYVESANT, BROOKLYN
104 SQUARE FEET

Viviana Olen and Matt Harkins started the
THNK1994 Museum in the hallway of their
railroad apartment. The subject matter? The
Tonya Harding/Nancy Kerrigan incident. In
part because of the tiny museum's colossal
success—and, in part, because they wanted
their apartment back—the BFFs have moved the
museum into a former hair salon in Bed-Stuy.

Viviana: "Our subject matter is very niche. The theme running throughout all the exhibits is how the media devours women in the public eye.

"We were roommates and best friends. We moved into an apartment in Williamsburg with a 23-foot-long hallway and no living room. We're like, 'We've got to do something with that hallway.'

"One winter night Matt watched the documentary called *The Price of Gold* on Netflix. It told the story of ice-skater Nancy Kerrigan getting clubbed in the leg by a hitman hired by the ex-husband of her archrival Tonya Harding. Matt's like, 'You've got to come home and watch this.' I was on a date. I was like, 'I'm on my way.' We became obsessed. It happened right before the Winter Olympics in 1994. We were only six and seven when it happened.

"Matt was working at the 9/11 museum at the time and he was upset because nobody there wanted to talk about Nancy and Tonya. I was like, 'A-la-la, Tonya and Nancy Museum!' We put it on Kick-

starter, and the response was insane. People wanted to not only revisit the story but to tell their stories."

Matt: "The museum was never ironic. We always treat the subjects with respect. We wanted to create a space for discussion because you're not stupid if you want to have a deep conversation about this, but also it's a little crazy, so you're having fun with it, too.

"The thing with Tonya was that she was so confident. Everything figure skaters were supposed to be, she rebelled against—the hair, make-up, costumes—and she had the goods to back it up. She was the first American to land the triple axel. But, because she never humbled herself in front of us, our response was to absolutely destroy her."

Viviana: "We recently showed a series of paintings by Laura Collins of the Olsen twins hiding from the paparazzi. You see them so aggressively hiding. They worked in the public eye from infancy to eighteen. They gave us so fucking much of themselves. Nothing is cooler than closing the gates and only appearing when they choose."

Matt: "Our day job is working at Sizzle Pie, a vegan pizza place. We're countergirls."

Viviana: "But we dedicate our lives to this. We live the museum lifestyle.

"A museum is really about facilitating community. It's never, 'Come here, and watch us do a show.' It's: 'Come here for discussion.' We did a Britney Spears panel. It was spiritual. It's such a small, intimate space that if anybody wants to talk, they can. You're in a room where nobody's sitting there judging you. You get to be a kid again. That's what I think museums are about."

23

UNOPPRESSIVE NON-IMPERIALIST BARGAIN BOOKS

BARGAIN BOOKSTORE

WEST VILLAGE, MANHATTAN

167½ SQUARE FEET

If you're looking for something penned by Newt Gingrich, Rush Limbaugh, or even Ayn Rand at this little bookstore with a big name, move on, because proprietor and revolutionary Jim Drougas has got nothing for you.

There will never be a Bob Dylan book that I refuse to sell. We're in the Village, so we get people from all over the world in tears because they get to see where Bob Dylan lived.

"There's not a lot of space, so I cultivate little pockets. But I'll have two shelves of William Blake because I love William Blake. Because, if you don't love William Blake, you have no business being in here, really.

"It's also partly about what I rule out. With rare exceptions, I will not sell books with very obnoxious religious content, especially for children. On the other hand, there was a cookbook called *What Would Jesus Eat*, and I thought that was hilarious. I couldn't resist.

"There was a point in time when I wouldn't mind so much selling Ayn Rand, but, in the face of the current Libertarian Republican revolution, I'm just like, no thanks. People do ask for her books but I just said, 'Nah, fuck her. I'm not selling her books anymore.'

"By having the wrong things on the shelf, I'm actually not helping society.

"Young people are much more hip nowadays. The sixties were just a dress rehearsal for the Occupy Movement. Occupy didn't fail because it was inept. It failed because it was fucked over with absolute precision and hammered to death by every police force, every FBI agent, every kind of subterfuge they could possibly think of. They can't allow young people to be that hip and that smart and accomplish that much. But, in fact, young people *are* that smart now. In the sixties, it was all about the war, civil rights. Those things are still important, but now it's all about the economy, and everyone's a fucking economist.

Young people are much

"When I first opened, I got a lot of people saying Unoppressive Non-Imperialist Bargain Books was a bad name because no one's gonna remember it. And it's true. People don't remember it, but they love it nonetheless. It's 'Unoppressive' in that our prices are so good they're not oppressive. We are saying 'Non-Imperialistic' not 'Anti-imperialistic'—even though we are anti-imperialistic. But it means that we're not Amazon or Barnes & Noble. We are not trying to take over the world.

"Twenty-five years ago, we took up two storefronts. It's a shell of what it was back in its heyday. I have three subtenants to make the rent. It's about survival. It's not even remotely about thriving.

"The rents here are crazy because there's always another sucker lied to by a broker who says: 'You're gonna make a fortune. This is the Village.'

"It's a big scam. Like Wall Street, which is just one giant pyramid scheme. The whole capitalist system is a pyramid scam, ultimately."

more hip nowadays.

24

GREENWICH LOCKSMITHS
LOCKSMITH
GREENWICH VILLAGE, MANHATTAN
125 SQUARE FEET

Philip Mortillaro cannot be described in one word, unless there is a term for locksmith-philosopher-artist-renegade-first-generation-family-man-wiseass-badass. Since 1980, he's been cutting keys and cracking safes out of his store, the smallest freestanding building in New York City.

> My parents were born in Sicily, and I was born on Elizabeth Street. I only went to school up to eighth grade. I was left back three times because I was a terror. It was just my nature. I did whatever I could to aggravate them. That was my sole occupation, and I did a good job of it. I'll never forget what the principal told me. He said, 'You're gonna be a burden to society.'

"The thing is, I have this trade. I've been locksmithing since I was fourteen. I've always had a shop. I've been employing people since I was eighteen years old. I never get bored of it. It's all about solving problems. You're working with puzzles.

"I have such a good reputation here. All of my keys work because I use a micrometer, which no one else does. It measures to the thousandth of an inch. You only have to be one ten thousandth of an inch off for a key not to work. That's the width of a piece of paper. I cut thousands and thousands of keys a week. And if I get one back it's a lot. Precision is the whole name of the game. Something we're lacking today is quality.

Keys are numbers, just like hacking is numbers.

"Keys are numbers, just like hacking is numbers. When you code computers, it's the same as setting up a master key system. My son is in the business with me. He does all the computer stuff for the electronic jobs. He's smart. He loves math. We all love math. Math is so true, so honest. It's always gonna be what it is.

"When I first bought this building, the owner wanted forty thousand dollars. I offered him twenty thousand dollars cash, and he took it like a thief in the night because he wasn't getting any money out of the place. A fortune-teller was in here that never paid rent. You gotta realize it was almost fifty years ago. That building across the street was empty, only gas stations here, cars and trucks all over the sidewalk. It was like hell. I liked it because it's where I belong. But not today—everything's so nice now. It's such bullshit. I don't need nice. It was working fine for me before.

"This is Disney World now. You go on a safari in Disney World, right? You wade through water, but there won't be any poisonous snakes. No

I don't need nice.

giant anything is gonna come out and get you because it's all plastic plants. That's what New York City is now. Fucking Disney World.

"I make metal sculptures. I decorated the store's facade with 10,000 keys, including a Van Gogh *The Starry Night* mural out of keys. Why? To bring some art and individuality back to the Village.

"The store is 125 square feet, and I use every square inch: drawers, counters, six machines, keys covering every wall, shelves all the way up the ceiling. I even have Sidney Solomon's ashes in a box in that corner up there. He worked for me for eighteen years. Thing with Sid was, he was a good friend of mine. So when Sid said, 'Phil, when I die I want my ashes thrown off the Brooklyn Bridge,' I said: 'Fine, I could do that for you.'

"But I hadn't been on the Brooklyn Bridge in a long time. You can't get to that outside ramp. So now I'm gonna be the Sicilian guy who looks Arab throwing white powder off a bridge. I have to put it on hold until, politically, it's a more suitable time. Until then, Sid's up there in the corner. He loved this shop. Sid worked all the time. Sid liked work—taught me a lot about business and life.

"I guess if you've been around long enough, you get philosophical. What

Nobody owns you.

are the really serious questions? It's just, 'Why the fuck are we here?' It's too horrible to contemplate. So you distract yourself with a Canada Goose jacket. But the real question is still there.

"Chase offered me 2 million dollars to buy the building to build an ATM. I turned them down. They came back with a better offer, and I said, 'Not interested.' They said, 'Do you even want to hear what it is?' I said, 'No, what do I want to hear it for? I'm not gonna sell it.'

That might even be the key to life.

"Because what am I gonna do with that money? I have everything I need, and that's a great way to live. Nobody owns you. That's how to get around in this society without having to put up with all the bullshit. That might even be the key to life."

25

VILLAGE BARBER SHOP
BARBERSHOP
CHELSEA, MANHATTAN
95 SQUARE FEET

Back in his native Tajikistan, Avi Jacobov's father owned a three-story barbershop with seventy-five barbers working for him. Today, at Avi's pint-size place on 22nd Street, customers wait for a trim in a chair on the sidewalk outside the shop.

❝ In Russia, my father had a small place, like this place. He worked for years. Then he found a big place. Step by step, he made the first floor for men, the second floor for women, and, on the third floor, he had a playground for kids.

"When I was young, my father would take me to the shop. I swept the floors. When I was nine, one customer said to my father, 'Listen. You know what? Tell your son to come cut my hair.' And my father said, 'No, no, no. He's just helping me. No, no, no.' He gave in and put out a chair for me to stand on, and I took the clippers. I gave him a buzz cut.

"In 1988, we had to leave and we only had one week to get out. We left everything. It was a big commotion. There was a corrupt revolution

and they started with the Anti-Semitism. We are Jews, so we moved to Israel.

"When you come to Israel, it's not easy. In Russia, I was the Jewish guy. In Israel, I was the Russian guy. I was like, 'What's going on here?'

"It took me three years to get in the swing of things. After serving in the Israeli military, I played the lottery and won a Green Card. My father's plan was always to come to America to make an American business, so I always thought about it. I came by myself. I knew zero English. I found a job in

Queens cutting hair. A few years later, I opened this place.

"I don't worry about small, because, for a barber, you only need space to pull the chair out. It's that simple. It's just a haircut, and that's it.

"In the summer, it's better because the people can wait outside on the chair. Winter is a little bit difficult.

"After two haircuts, I come up with a customer nickname. That customer waiting outside? He used to be Blondie Boy. But now he's married. So he's just Blondie. I have a Chelsea Boy, a James Bond. My nickname is Avi Baba.

"I'm also matchmaker. Sometimes the customers say, 'I'm alone. You have a nice customer?' I say, 'OK. I find for you next boyfriend.' Sometimes the customer's in my chair, another customer is sitting outside. The one in the chair says, 'Oh, he's so handsome.' I say, 'Oh, you like him?' He says, 'Yes.' I say, 'OK, I'm going to talk to him.' They get together. It's that easy. Sometimes it works out, but the problem is, if they fight together, they don't want to sit next to each other waiting for a haircut. One disappears, one stays. Not good for business."

I don't worry about small

26

MINI PAAN SHOP
AFTER-DINNER TREAT
JACKSON HEIGHTS, QUEENS
40 SQUARE FEET

Paan is made of a fresh leaf wrapped around dried fruits, nuts, and pastes, and is chewed widely across parts of Asia. To the uninitiated, it's like a cross between chewing tobacco and those colorful fennel seed snacks found at the cash registers of Indian restaurants. To its detractors, paan is an addictive stimulant with adverse health effects. But Musleh Uddin, owner of the Mini Paan Shop, swears by its many benefits.

You're chewing on a fresh leaf. It's called *betel leaf*. Inside is the betel nut and other different things. There are three kinds of paan: sweet, normal, and tobacco.

"They're a dollar or two each. The juice comes out, and you can swallow it or spit it out. It makes your mouth red. In Bangladesh, my mom, my father, everyone chewed it. It's a tradition.

"They grow the trees in Ohio and Florida. It comes in on a plane, and people deliver it in a truck. My customers are from Bangladesh, India, Pakistan, Nepal, Arabia, and America; a few Spanish people. It's a gathering place for people. I'm open twenty-four hours. A lot of cab drivers come at three in the morning. So it's not a boring place to work.

"The shop is the size of an elevator but it's not about size. What I depend on is luck. If God wants to give you something, He will give it to you. You have to have faith.

"The paan is very helpful. Physical-wise and mental-wise, everything goes up. Some people are in a bad mental state—and it really helps them. When you are focusing on chewing, your mind doesn't go to other things.

"Also, it helps the body, like Vitamin C. And, if you don't mind me saying, it's good for the love life. Also, you chew it after a big meal, and it freshens yours breath and helps digestion.

"The first time people try it, they say, 'Ugh, disgusting!' It's big, and you have to put the whole thing in your mouth. Some people say it tastes like candy, grass, spices, flowers, soap. Once you start chewing and get used to it, you like it.

"It's not really addictive—depends on your mind. It's up to you. I chew one every hour. But I could stop. Ramadan is coming, right? We can't chew. And nothing happens.

"I love America with all my heart, honestly. We don't call it the land of opportunity for nothing. It's part of what I am now, because, if I was still back home in Bangladesh, I don't know what I would be.

"I have three daughters and I'm taking them back to Bangladesh next month for the first time. I want them to know the culture. Even if you're born and bred over here, you need to know where you're from. Basically, every country is the same. Culture is the only difference. Otherwise, everything's the same. We're all human beings."

27

THE LUNGTA
HOUSEBOAT
CITY ISLAND, THE BRONX

35 FEET

Gigmy Bista hails from the landlocked
nation of Nepal. He lives on a fishing boat
but doesn't fish. His boat has a motor, but
he's never turned it on. Yet, somehow it all
makes beautiful, poetic, perfect sense.

" I grew up in Nepal, which has no oceans. My parents think it's weird I live on a boat because in Nepal, we only have little rowboats. The village in the Himalayas where I grew up is one of the highest human settlements in the world. No road and stuff like that.

"I came here in 2006 to study. I have a degree in Economics, but I haven't done anything related to that. Now I deal in Nepalese handicrafts.

"My girlfriend, Jing, and I came to City Island to hang out with a friend who had a boat. We immediately liked it because of the nature— nature below us, nature above us. Nobody disturbs you. It's a small space inside the boat, but it's like your backyard is the whole world.

"We named the boat Lungta, which means 'Windhorse' in Tibetan. It's a vintage 1960 Egg Harbor fishing boat. It cost about four grand. It's not very seaworthy. The motor works, but I never turned it on because I don't need to go anywhere. I just wanted it as a home. I don't fish because I'm Buddhist, and I can't bring myself to slice open a live fish.

"We have Wi-Fi, but you can't look at a screen when the boat's rocking. We go to the library to do work. We have a bathroom onboard, but we go to the church a lot because their better bathroom is better.

nature below us, nature above us

"The shower situation works for me but not so much for my girlfriend. It's a big plastic container with a pump. I dive into the ocean and stand on the stern, and Jing pumps the water. It's never warm. We have a membership at the gym and can shower there anytime we want.

"We joke that we both have 'boat-ready hair.' She has dreads, and I don't have any hair.

"All of it reminds me of home. Onboard, we have a space heater and a lot of warm blankets. In Nepal, every house has one fireplace and we use yak skin blankets. Here, we don't have a fridge onboard, so we go food shopping on daily basis. We didn't have a refrigerator back home either, because it's so cold you don't need one. We don't have running water on the boat, so I take the rowboat to the dock to fill the tank. Back home, my mom used to go to river for water. That's how it was.

"So this isn't really that hard. In fact, it's kind of luxurious compared to back home."

28

7 TRAIN
BALCONY TO SUBWAY DISTANCE
WOODSIDE, QUEENS

9½ FEET

Tasnova Faruque is raising her two toddlers in an apartment whose balcony is a basketball hoop's distance away from the 7 Flushing Local train. Yeah, it's loud, and, yeah, sometimes she sees commuters kissing or peering into her window. But she will tell you in her native Bengali, *"eta kono byapar ii noy"*—"it's no big deal."

" I came to America because it gives opportunity to people from other countries to do something better. Whatever you want to do here, you can do it.

"My husband and I came in April 2008. It was my first time leaving Bangladesh. My English was not good. We could only earn a little money, so everything was difficult. I didn't know about anything, not the streets or where we were going to live. But then God made it really easy for us. We found a house to live in, and we found a job.

"I took the GED. The test was not too hard because I did college for two years in my country. I did a customer care job in the Port Authority Bus Terminal for four years. After having the baby, I quit from the job to stay home.

"My husband was a medical doctor in my country. He took the GED and then studied for the exam you take to get the medical license. He studied a lot, but then he stopped. What could we do? We have to pay for the rent and the food, and I have to send the money to my country. They are back home waiting, you know?

"He took the exam for police officer and passed. He's in the 34th Precinct in the Bronx, near Yankee Stadium.

"When we first saw this apartment, it was very nice but very close to the subway, and the sound made us crazy. But then there was a lot of sunshine coming inside. It's easy for my husband to get to work. He hears the subway coming, throws his pants on and runs out, and in two minutes he's on the train.

"For me, the sound is worse in the night. Everything is quiet, then the train comes running so fast, and it makes a really bad sound. In the daytime, you cannot hear it much because of the TV, fan, the babies—everything.

"The babies go out on the balcony and play in the rain and the snow. Sometimes, if the rain is hard and the train goes by fast, they get soaked. They love it. They have their own amusement park outside.

"In the morning I see people run for the train with the coffee in their hand. At night my husband and I sit on the balcony, and we can see lot of beautiful hugs and warm kisses and love with the couples on the platform. It's like watching a movie. Sometimes people see us inside and wave and say, 'Hi!' and I say, 'Yeah, sure. Hi, hi!' But then I got a big sheet to cover our bedroom window."

29

RONALD TORREYES
A.K.A. "TOE"
NY YANKEE

YANKEE STADIUM, SOUTH BRONX

5 FEET 8 INCHES, 151 POUNDS

Ronald Torreyes can be described as a pint-size utility man, a diminutive infielder, or *enano*, the Spanish term for "pipsqueak." But one thing's for sure. The New York Yankees' littlest player has a big bat at the plate and a big glove in the field.

Definitely, there were a lot of people who told me you're not gonna make it because you don't have the height. There were a lot of teams that wouldn't look at me, that wouldn't give me a chance.

"But my dad was always there for me. He kept encouraging me and said that, if I keep training hard, someone would give me an opportunity. He said, 'Keep working and eventually you'll get the chance to show them you can play.'

"My dad had baseball in his blood. I guess at a young age he saw something in me and he dedicated himself to my training. When I was growing up, we used to train twice a day: in the morning, then I would study, then train again at night. Even on weekends.

"To me, it was faraway, the chance to be a professional player, but I worked really hard with my dad, and now I'm here. I'm in the big leagues.

"It shows kids that if you work really hard at what you want to do, you can accomplish it. Nothing is impossible in life when you work for it every day. Young players can look at me and see that if you will it—and you work for it—you can do it. I would tell kids to never lose faith in themselves and to keep working every day.

"Being shorter makes me quicker than the other guys. I'm faster than the bigger players. I play different positions—second base, third base, shortstop, and right field—and speed is an advantage in all those places.

"If I had to say a disadvantage of my size, it would be the same thing I encountered early in my career. That people would dismiss me because of my stature. But I'm very, very thankful to the Yankees for giving me the opportunity to show that I can really play this sport.

"Being a New York Yankee means so much me. Being on this team is something I carry in my heart. So many legends have passed through here, retired or gone. That's what makes you give everything you have. It's an extra boost of energy you get just from wearing this uniform. You wear it with honor.

"There's a special handshake I have with [outfielder] Aaron Judge. He's a foot taller than I am and 100 pounds heavier. He puts his hand up high, and I jump up and high-five him. We do it at the beginning of the game or after a big play. It goes to show you, he's so big and I'm so little and, yet at the same time, we're on the same team giving it all we've got."

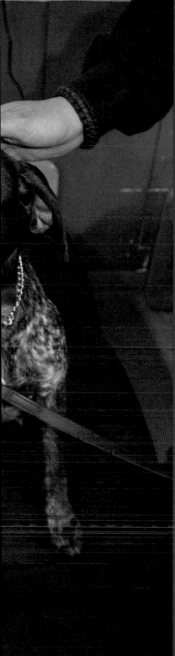

30

SULLY
BOMB-SNIFFING POLICE DOG
NYPD TRANSIT CANINE UNIT
LONG ISLAND CITY, QUEENS
46 POUNDS

Half the size of a typical police dog, Sully
may be the smallest canine on the force, but
the German Shorthaired Pointer's got a big
responsibility—sniffing out bombs. Officer
Kevin Belavsky explains why Sully's German
Shepherd colleagues have got nothing on him.

Sully looks for explosives. He's an explosive detection dog. What he does is very confidential, so we can't go into details. He's got a very good nose. His drive is unbelievable. He's a feisty little one. You would have to say he is like the Tasmanian devil because all he wants to do is work, work, work, and run, run, run. Psychotic, you know? But not aggressive at all. He's such a friendly dog.

"He doesn't have a Napoleon complex, but he does bark a lot. He's a pointing dog. They're very big duck dogs. He used to chase squirrels and birds, but he's getting better. He's a little bit older now so his work drive is there. When he's in search mode, he's in search mode.

"I used to work in Anti-Crime in Brooklyn North's transit unit. To be in K9, it's a dream come true. I did CrossFit for a solid year to train to get into the unit because I love animals. It's very intense. It's a very elite unit. It's a tight unit. It's a totally different job. You're glued to an animal. You're with the dog more than you're with your family.

"Sully's a year old and full grown, so he's in training now. We have to make sure the dog is capable of working in the New York City subway system. You have loud noises, crowds, elevators, escalators, trains. You've got to make sure this dog isn't scared of the public. Some dogs do wash out, unfortunately. They don't have what it takes. Then that dog goes back to wherever they got it from.

"Sully will work everywhere—all five boroughs: He'll work the streets, what we call 'topside.' And he'll work underground on the subway. That's what we call 'the hole.'

"You have to have full confidence in your dog. In this day and age, terrorism is huge. The Transit K9 team trains for any and every eventuality. When he's out in play, the presumption is something's going to happen. We are not there in this metaphorical world. We are there because we have a responsibility to prepare for real threats. It's a tremendous

deterrent for the bad guys to know this dog exists. Should someone do something, the ability for him to save lives quickly is huge.

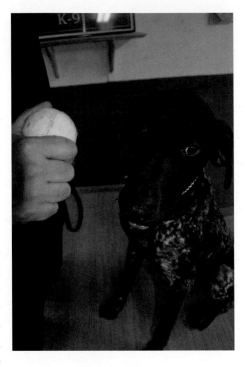

"People ask me if I love him, and I explain it's a tool on your belt. It's not a house pet, it's my work dog. I trust him. You don't love. Yeah, I love coming to work, but he's my tool. He's my firearm on my side.

"You're not going to go home and let him run around your house because when you need him to do the work, he has to do the work. If you treat him like a tool and you put him in the kennel, when you take him out that dog is ready to work. I have two kids and my wife. The dog has no interaction with the family.

"He's my partner, the best partner. He doesn't talk back. He doesn't change the radio in the patrol car. He doesn't eat on the job. He won't hurry you when he's hungry. I drink coffee. He drinks water. The only thing he will do is tell you he's got to go to the bathroom. He'll empty out when he has to. When you give that dog that command to empty, he'll go."

In the tradition of naming police dogs after fallen officers, Sully is named after Lieutenant Tom Sullivan, a thirty-eight-year veteran of the force and president of the Lieutenants Benevolent Association, who died in 2012.

31

HYPACROSAURUS ALTISPINUS (JUVENILE)
DINOSAUR
UPPER WEST SIDE, MANHATTAN
LENGTH: 20 INCHES/WIDTH: 3 INCHES/HEIGHT: 8 INCHES

The American Museum of Natural History has one of the world's greatest dinosaur fossil collections. Yet, some of the 5 million visitors passing through each year might be passing by one of the littlest dinosaurs in the place. Dr. Mark Norell, the curator and chief of the museum's paleontology division, explains how *Hypacrosaurus altispinus* isn't the only little dinosaur we may be overlooking.

This little guy was a year old. It would have grown to 25 feet long and walked on four limbs but was also capable of walking on two for short distances. It was herbivorous and lived about 7 million years ago.

"But the truth is, the smallest dinosaur isn't even in this hall. It's the bumblebee hummingbird from Cuba, which weighs 2 grams and can perch on the edge of a pin. That's because birds are living dinosaurs. Dinosaurs aren't extinct. Birds are a kind of dinosaur just like humans are a kind of primate. Pretty much all dinosaurs had feathers.

"This is a fairly new theory, and it takes a while for things to percolate into popular culture, but people are starting to get it. They probably evolved feathers in the same way we use down jackets—as a thermal

barrier to the environment. It was a pre-adaptation to the flight that came later.

"So, technically speaking, *Hypacrosaurus altispinus* is our smallest *non-avian* dinosaur. People have this idea dinosaurs were all really big because, at the turn of the century, all the major museums sent people out to find giant dinosaurs to fill their giant halls. Also, small animals don't preserve well because their bones are more delicate.

"Finding young dinosaur bones used to be extremely rare, but in the last four decades lots have been found in North America and Central Asia. All the dinosaurs I work on are very small because we can't excavate large things in remote areas of Mongolia, for example. There's no access to heavy equipment, so we only collect what we can put into the trucks.

"In the sixties and early seventies, science for the general public was two things: outer space and Jacques Cousteau. Later, the fascination transferred to dinosaurs. Some people say that's because of the *Jurassic Park* movie, but I disagree. I think that movie was a business opportunity that capitalized on this fomenting interest in dinosaurs.

"People today are saying you shouldn't encourage more kids to be scientists or paleontologists. The problem is science is expensive, and there's just not enough money. What we need are more kids to become engineers and to code. But what we *really* need is a much more science-literate public. So when you hear crackpot stuff like global warming isn't happening, it will be rejected.

"So I always feel that if, when visitors leave the museum, they've learned two or three things—then I'm totally happy."

Dr. Mark Norell is the Macaulay Curator in the Division of Paleontology and the division's chair, American Museum of Natural History.

32

VABA EESTI SÕNA
(FREE ESTONIAN WORD)
NEWSPAPER
MURRAY HILL, MANHATTAN
CIRCULATION: 1,000

Starting in World War II, the small Baltic republic of Estonia was occupied by the Soviets, the Germans, and then the Soviets again until it finally achieved its independence after the fall of the Berlin Wall. Throughout it all, a scrappy little Estonian newspaper has been rolling off the presses in New York City. Editor-in-chief Kärt Ulman gives the inside scoop.

The paper was established after our homeland was occupied by Soviet Russia. The first edition was printed on June 1, 1949. It disclosed the horrible news to the world that the Soviets had deported tens of thousands of Estonians to Siberia in cattle cars in one night. The few Estonian-language newspapers that sprung up in the free world were literally the only 'free words' of Estonia. That's why the paper's called the *Free Estonian Word*.

"After the second World War, a big wave of Estonians arrived in the U.S., mostly from displaced persons camps in Germany. They fled Estonia in fear of the Russians coming back after the Germans left.

"The refugees here needed a newspaper to connect them to the Estonian community spread out all over the U.S. They needed a channel to cheer them up and to give them hope for a better future.

"The paper was also a very important cultural platform for intellectuals. You see, Estonians coming here were mostly highly educated people who had to work in low-level jobs. They couldn't express themselves as they once did in their previous lives. The only way to express themselves on their intellectual level and in their native language was by publishing articles in the newspaper.

"Now *Free Estonian Word* is the only Estonian-language newspaper in America. Our circulation has dropped considerably—it was around 5,000 in the 1960s. Right now the number is 1,000. It's a weekly paper with about a dozen pages. I am convinced the paper ties the community together and is needed for a healthy Estonian subculture to flourish. The paper's survival is the very issue right now.

"My title is editor-in-chief, but, actually, I'm the only editor. I collect material, write, edit, and translate. I do the layout and edit the photos.

"I hope most Americans know where Estonia is by now. Maybe they know we invented Skype? Or they've heard Estonia has the highest supermodel per capita of any country in the world. Why? I guess we are the perfect blend of Nordic people and the many nationalities that conquered us over centuries. So we have had just the right amount of foreign blood to make us stronger and more attractive but not enough to make us disappear.

"Americans might also know that we won our independence from the Soviet Union in the Singing Revolution. We had mass demonstrations with spontaneous singing of national songs that were forbidden during the Soviet occupation.

"If Estonian people had to give advice to the U.S. about dealing with Russia, we would say, 'Be careful. Check the facts. Make sure you are covered. Be strong and confident—Russians respect power.'"

33

DALILA'S PET WEAR
DOGGIE COUTURE

JACKSON HEIGHTS, QUEENS

SIZE: XS (YORKIE)–XXL (LABRADOR)

If your dog has a prom, quinceañera, or red carpet event coming up, Miguel Rodriguez is your man. The fashion designer makes miniature-size formalwear for pets that's over-the-top and completely fabulous.

I come from this very small town in Mexico called San Juan Colón. I didn't fit it in. I was not the macho man—tall with the hairy chest and dark skin—that would carry bags of maize and throw it in the back of the truck.

"I was the youngest of seven. I was not allowed to cook—and I love to cook. I was not allowed to clean. I was not allowed to play with dolls. But my mom allowed me to sew simple things on the machine, and I learned the basics.

"We had this parade every year called *Reina de la Primavera*—Queen of the Spring. Everyone would sew the fanciest things. When the parade passed by, I was like, 'Oh my God. I want to be *La Reina*!' *Reina de la Primavera* fit me perfectly. I was always a curvy, chubby guy, but I have a beautiful smile. People say my smile is one of my gifts. I'm always cheering people up. I try with my heart to not put down people, because I was put down a lot. Never underestimate the power of your words.

"I told my mom, 'The *Reina de la Primavera* needs a prince.' She said, 'No, you're crazy!' But all I thought was, 'How can I get into that truck with the princess?' Then there went Miguel! I ran off and jumped in, and a star was born. The next year I was the prince, and I made my own outfit.

"When I first came to New York I was seventeen, and my English was very basic. I didn't want to work in a factory, but there was nothing else. We would work fourteen hours a day for five dollars an hour at a recycling center. They give

a star was born.

you a mask, gloves, glasses. It was summer. There was garbage, dead animals, food decomposing. I felt nauseous all the time and couldn't eat. I would take a shower and still smell it.

"After that, I worked for years bussing tables and finally became a server. Years pass. No sewing. No nothing. Then my ex-boyfriend gave me Venus, my first dog, as a birthday gift. She's a Miniature Schnauzer. It changed everything. I wasn't prepared for the responsibility. I worked long hours and would make her pee on the pads or just wait. I didn't know better. One busy day at work, I was holding my pee for like thirty minutes, and it hit me: This is exactly how she feels.

"I told my boss I was leaving and ran home and told Venus, 'You don't deserve this.' I switched shifts so she could go out when she needed to.

"For Venus's first birth-day party, I wanted a nice dress for her—a princess dress—like *Reina de la Primavera*. I look, but there was nothing. So I bought a sewing machine and made one. It was horrible. Venus ended up being Lady Godiva and going naked. But I kept at it and finally created my first dress for her, just a sim-ple summer dress. Plain. Nothing fancy. Flower-ish, obviously.

"Then Venus needed a haircut. I took her to Petco

but didn't like it. I tried those fancy groomers you see on TV. Then I went out and bought the clippers to do it myself. I loved it, and my hubby told me, 'Why don't you go to school for it?' I quit my job and took the course. It was my dream come true. I was the wife. He was working. I had a kid. I could just make freaking dresses all day and rescue dogs. I started shaving the rescues and that led to me opening up Venus & Dalila Pet Spa, which does grooming.

"Because people knew about Venus and her dresses, I started doing doggie fashion shows in the gay bars to fundraise for shelters. Then I entered the New York Pet Fashion Show. My stuff got a lot of publicity: interviews, pictures, newspapers, magazines. I was not expecting it. Interviews. In 2014, I created Dalila's Pet Wear.

My style is based in my roots.

"I was doing things differently than other designers. We're Latinos, so I started dressing doggies in Mexican *fútbol* shirts, *puebla* shirts, Frida Kahlo-inspired outfits. My style is based in my roots: *Reina de la Primavera*.

"My customers go from very basic everyday people, just like me, to big stars. But there are no regular people in my world. That's the whole thing. There is nothing more sincere than a dog's love. You can see it through their eyes. They don't demand anything except love. And pretty dresses."

34

TWIG TERRARIUMS

TERRARIUMS

GOWANUS, BROOKLYN

2 INCHES AND UP

What do you get when you cross a lifelong plant nerd and a cerebral poet? You get Twig, a business that makes mossy microcosms in terrariums. Michelle Inciarrano and Katy Maslow are co-owners and besties whose business titles are the same: "Half-a-Twig."

Michelle: "I'm a wacko. I've always been into plants. In kindergarten, you know how you use toothpicks to plant a potato? Well, my potato grew taller than me, and I became afraid of it. My parents had to get rid of it."

Katy: "I have a degree in poetry. Every terrarium is a little tiny narrative with a little tiny story being told. They're all little poems."

Michelle: "It all started with this magical cruet jar I fell in love with. I said, 'I'm going to make a terrarium in this.'"

Katy: "I had never heard the word *terrarium*. After she put the moss in it, it looked like a little garden, so I thought it needed little people. We started making our own little people, and, before we knew it, we had terrariums all over our houses."

Michelle: "We started selling them from a booth at Brooklyn Flea, and the response was incredible. Our terrariums range from easy to care for to more complex."

Katy: "A lot of people roll in here claiming they're a black thumb. We play plant matchmaker. We connect the people, their lighting conditions, and maintenance capabilities with the right plants for them. We see a lot of windows that face train stations in Brooklyn, and that's what inspired us—bringing life into places where it would not otherwise be. As they say, a tree grows in Brooklyn."

Michelle: "We don't really have gardens in the city so terrariums allow people to have this little microcosm of greenery to care for.

"We do bucolic scenes of yogis by waterfalls and sheep grazing on verdant rolling hills, but we also do some pretty out-there stuff. For a creepy holiday gift guide, we made a really graphic *CSI* crime investigation scene with a dead body and detectives logging evidence."

Katy: "We try to represent life, death, and everything in between.

Michelle: "We got contacted to make a terrarium for Martin Scorsese. I lost my mind. I said, 'What do you want inside of it?' They said, 'You're the artist, you decide.' So we picked the cornfield scene in *Casino* with the mobsters beating Joe Pesci's brother to death with baseball bats. We sent them pictures, and they said, 'It's a little too much.' So we did something too gory for Martin Scorsese, OK?"

Michelle: "We've known each other forever. We were little punk hooligans cutting school and listening to heavy metal."

Katy: "We were troubled youths. So we connected on that level of being young and on our own."

Katy: "This is absolutely like a marriage, and Twig is our bizarre baby."

Michelle: "At the end of the day, we can't complain."

Katy: "We get to make fucking terrariums together. Think about that."

Michelle: "It's like being seven years old with your bestie and just doing something great."

THE SUN

by

Harry Crosby

Black Sun Press
Rue Cardinale
Paris
1929

35

THE SUN BY HARRY CROSBY
LIBRARY BOOK
NEW YORK PUBLIC LIBRARY MAIN BRANCH
MIDTOWN, MANHATTAN
1 INCH BY ¾ INCH

The New York Public Library's Rare Books
Division is stacked with astounding works. The
collection includes the *Gutenberg Bible*, the only
surviving copy of Columbus's letter from 1493
announcing his encounter with the New World,
and the original handwritten manuscript of Oscar
Wilde's *The Importance of Being Earnest*. Michael
Inman, the library's Curator of Rare Books,
talks about the tiniest book in the
enormous collection—the only one you
need a magnifying glass to read.

"Our classification for miniature books is that the height of the spine is less than three inches tall. It's a bit of an arbitrary distinction. We have about 2,000 of them. They've been around for centuries. They were printed then—as is the case now—as novelty items. When you go up to the counter in Barnes & Noble and they have a spindle rack with little books, it's the same thing—something unique and quaint.

"*The Sun* by Harry Crosby is our smallest book. Only one hundred copies were printed in 1929. The binding is Moroccan leather with a little gold sun on the cover. It was handset in three-point type. That means each letter is only a millimeter in height.

"It's a prose poem—a meditation on why he deified the sun. Crosby today is not remembered for his writing. He's remembered for his wild lifestyle and his talent for spotting writing talent.

"He was born into the upper crust of Boston society. His uncle was J.P. Morgan. He had everything laid out for him, but he volunteered to serve in the ambulance corps in World War I. He had a romantic sense of war. But he witnessed war's gruesome nature and the carnage on the Western Front. It affected not just his sense of himself but his broader place in the world. He came back home to a world he was no longer part of and that's why he left to live a life abroad in Paris.

"He threw off all the old conventions and reinvented himself. He became a bon vivant and a bohemian—drugs and sex, basically. He had an open relationship with his wife. Together, they founded the Black Sun Press. They were the first to publish authors who, back then, were unknown and struggling: James Joyce, Hemingway, D. H. Lawrence, T. S. Eliot, Ezra Pound.

"The last couple of years of his life he spiraled out of control. He died at thirty-one in a suicide pact with a lover. It was a huge scandal. People who knew him said that sui-cide was the ultimate new experience for him. He was definitely one of these peo-ple who was not destined to make old bones.

"There was talk of it being a murder-suicide. The coro-ner said Crosby died several hours after the woman. The odd thing is, he was con-stantly writing to chronicle his emotions. Yet, he didn't write a single word while he was sitting there for hours in a room with a dead person. He didn't even leave a sui-cide note."

36

CYLINDER SEAL: HUNTING SCENE CIRCA 2250–2150 BC

ANCIENT ARTIFACT

THE METROPOLITAN MUSEUM OF ART
UPPER EAST SIDE, MANHATTAN
HEIGHT: 1½ INCH

The crowds at The Met may flock to the
colossal Temple of Dendur or the towering
Sphinx of Hatshepsut, but Yelena Rakic, the
associate curator of ancient Near Eastern
art, is fixated on the cylinder seal, which is
about as big as the tip of your thumb.

" I grew up in Manhattan, and I came to the museum all the time as a child. What drew me in the most were the Impressionist paintings. I'm not embarrassed to say it.

"There is so much to see at the Met and cylinder seals are so small that some people just walk by them. The Cylinder Seal Hunting Scene is the smallest object in the *The Metropolitan Museum of Art Guide*—a 450-page book with 600 works of art.

"It's hard to explain what a cylinder seal is. It's not something that's easy to convey at a cocktail party. When I say I study seals, people think it's the animal.

"At the simplest level, if you think about the phrase 'to seal,' it means to secure something. A stamp on a document is a seal. The difference is the cylinder seal is carved and, instead of being used on paper, it's rolled onto clay, leaving behind an impression. Also, the seal can go on infinitely because, as the seal is rolled, the design it makes repeats.

"Seals had two different functions: One was authenticating documents. Documents in those days were clay tablets inscribed with Cuneiform. The authority verifying those documents would impress his seal on the tablets—like a notary public.

"The second function is that seals were impressed on lumps of clay used to secure doors and lids of storage jars for things like barley or wheat. The impressions identified the owner and protected against unauthorized opening.

"They were also believed to have protective amulet properties, so people wore them as jewelry and were even buried with them.

"Also, they are beautiful. The Hunting Scene seal is one of the masterpieces in the collection. It's such a balanced composition. You have the hunter grasping this horned animal. You have these fir trees and mountains—a complete landscape. It has an inscription so we know who owned this seal. His name was Balu-ili. His profession was cupbearer, so he was a high-ranking officer for the royalty.

"We don't know that much about how seals were made. It's fascinating to think about how

they carved this tiny cylindrical object with these incredibly detailed miniature scenes. On top of that, the image is carved below the surface, so it creates a raised image when it's pressed. Everything is in reverse. This was four thousand years ago. There was no electricity, no power tools, no magnification. There is this whole range of how hard it must have been to make these things.

"What I love most is just being able to share my passion for something that is from a part of the world people only think awful things about. I think it's important to point out what has come out of the Middle East."

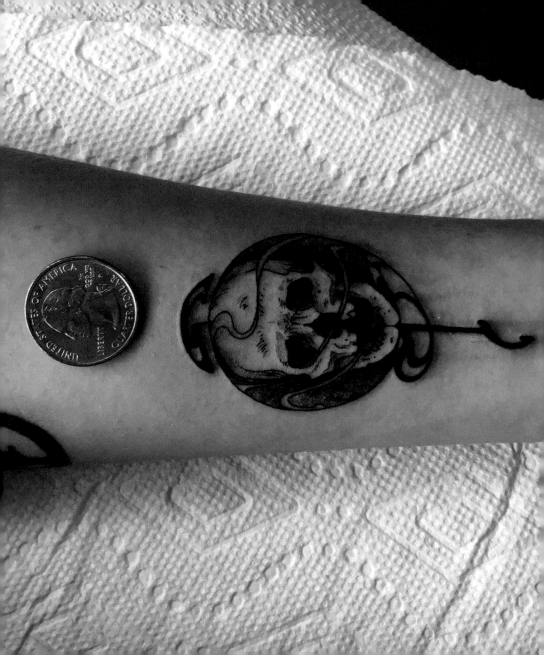

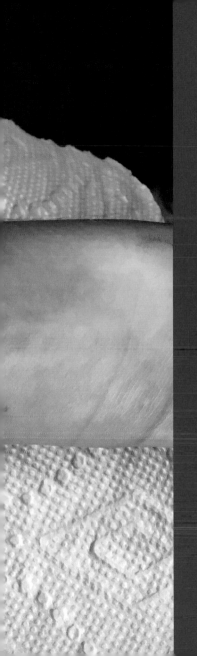

37

EAST SIDE INK
TATTOO
EAST VILLAGE, MANHATTAN

.955-2 INCHES

Making the perfect tiny tattoo means facing big challenges. It's easy to fix mistakes on a big, detailed tattoo. Not the case with small ones, where gaffes a millimeter in size are magnified. But Gerald Feliciano, a tattoo artist known for his quarter-size canvases, comes at the task with a steady hand.

There's absolutely not much room for error with a tiny tattoo. It is no secret that tattoos are never perfect; it never goes according to plan, ever. As a tattooer you just get better at fixing things. With a small tattoo, you have no room to mess up.

"I've given a lot of thought to how to make the tiny tattoo flawless—how to place the black, how to situate the negative space, and how to align the grey values. The goal is to provide contrast and ensure the image itself is recognizable.

it never goes according to plan, ever.

"I try to keep them the size of a quarter or slightly larger. Too small and it could blur out when it's older. Also, you can't do a face or words on that small a canvas. It can't be too detailed. It needs to be something that, from a distance, you can tell what it is.

"I do all kinds of tattoos, not just small ones. The most important thing is that they fit the person's aesthetic. When I first started out, I worked in the Bronx off of Fordham Road. It was a very street shop area.

"The first thing I'd do to gauge someone's aesthetic was to look at their shoes. The shoes tell you how they carry themselves. Back then, it was a lot of script names. A lot of gang stuff. There wasn't too much room for creativity. They wanted the cookie-cutter cholo-style stuff.

But working in an urban setting got me to learn the technical aspects and how to work efficiently. Because if you didn't take a walk-in right away, they'd go down the block to someone else and you were not going to make any money that day.

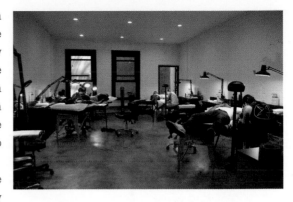

"It's hard to describe my aesthetic because I try to be as prolific as I can. I do a lot of Art Nouveau and Art Deco-style tattooing. Alphonse Mucha, Gustav Klimt, Aubrey Beardsley—those are my favorite artists. I do a lot of black and gray realism—painterly Caravaggio-type stuff.

"The first tiny tattoo I did was a swallow. Usually, I would turn something like that away. On that particular day I must have needed rent money. After that, I started designing tiny, ornamental brooch-like designs. There's something gratifying in starting and completing something in forty five minutes.

"I feel like smaller tattoos are often more personal. They're more meaningful, like a portrait of an animal that passed away. The person doesn't want a giant, gaudy-ass tattoo of it, but something more like a keepsake, something that's always there, this tiny, well-done piece. It's more intimate—it's more for you than it is for the world."

38

ALAN WOLFSON
MINIATURE URBAN SCULPTURES
HOLLIS TAGGART GALLERIES
CHELSEA, MANHATTAN
⅛ INCH=1 FOOT SCALE

Artist Alan Wolfson takes one of the world's
most massive cities, empties it of its people,
and condenses it to its grittiest core. His pieces
are astonishingly realistic but fictionalized
dioramas of a bygone New York whose
meaning must be construed by the viewer.
Just make sure to look closely or risk missing
a miniscule clue that unlocks the real story.

66 I want the viewer to get involved in what they're looking into. I want them to come up with a scenario of what happened here: Why is that sandwich on the counter only half-eaten? Is there a tip on the table? What's with those stomped-out cigarette butts by the subway entrance?

"I try to tell a story with these minute details. My work is not about how small everything is but the stories these small things tell. I don't put in people because 3-inch-tall people remind you you're looking at a miniature. I want you to be thinking about the narrative. One-foot in real life is ½-inch in my pieces so the environments are intricate. And, because the scale is so small, it's intimate.

"For many years, hardly any artists were working in miniature, and I felt my work wasn't being taken seriously as an artist. Only painting and sculpting were considered real art. I consider myself to be a

sculptor. My work is considered hyperrealism. Now, with more people working in miniature, it's taken more seriously. For me, it's always been the way of doing my work.

"I grew up in Brooklyn in the 1950s. My father worked as a commercial artist as a letterer and sign painter. In school, we had to build a diorama in a shoebox for homework. I loved that. I made scenes of what I saw on my walk to school: butcher shop, police station, that kind of thing. That's essentially what I'm still doing. I just kind of got carried away with it.

"I was a pretty rebellious kid. Then Vietnam came, and I was one of those hippies that got drafted. I saw so many lives get ruined. To cope, I started thinking about the New York City I grew up in and longed for. It removed me from the reality I was in. I said to myself, 'When I get out of this situation, I'm going to build a diorama of a subway station.'

"I make every element by hand in my pieces—all the lighting, the props and the architecture. I'll think about the piece for a long time,

visualizing, problem-solving. By the time I start, I've thought about it for months—years, maybe. I make a rough sketch to refresh my memory. I do research and pull photographs. Then I build a cardboard mock-up mainly to figure out sightlines. Then I replace the cardboard pieces with acrylic plastic. Some of these locations never actually existed. I make them up. I also make up 75 percent of the narrative as I go along and build the appropriate things to tell the story.

"People ask me why I always do environments with graffiti. It tells part of the story. When I went away to Vietnam in 1968, there was no such thing as graffiti. The first time I saw it when I came back from the service I thought, 'Well, it's kind of a mess, and I kind of like it.' I want it known that graffiti was part of the character of New York at that time.

Well, it's kind of a mess, and I kind of like it.

"I live in California. When I go back to New York it's changed so drastically I don't even feel like I'm in New York. I have fond memories of walking around 42nd Street when I was a teenager. Maybe it wasn't the nicest place in the world, but it was my place, and I felt comfortable there.

"I had a meeting a few years ago with the Times Square Alliance about doing a commission. I said to the guy, 'I have a question. Why the fuck did you screw up Times Square?' His eyes got big and his mouth dropped open. He said, 'We had to clean it up. Mayor Giuliani this and that…' And I said, 'You didn't do it for New Yorkers. It's a place where tourists buy T-shirts and postcards, like Main Street in Disneyland. You didn't clean anything up. You moved it on and made it someone else's problem and found a way to make money off of the place it had been.'

"Needless to say, I didn't get the commission.

"New York was more interesting back then. More genuine. People wanted to scribble on the subway so they did. If they wanted to vomit in the subway because they snorted too much heroin, they did. What I do is an accurate representation of New York, whether you like it or not."

39

E

FIRST NAME
CHELSEA, MANHATTAN
ONE LETTER

E Harper Nora Jeremijenko-Conley's first name is E, and it's always capitalized, and there's no period after the E. (Note: There was only a period right there because it was the end of a sentence.)

Some people might think of me as lowercase 'e,' but I feel very specific about it. A lowercase 'e' is so little, and it doesn't have those three straight lines.

"My parents thought of a lot of names that started with E before I was born. Like 'Early' because I was born two months early, but they decided to just name me E. They told me when I got older I could change it to any name that starts with E. But it's very hard to rename yourself. I can't see myself as, like, an Elizabeth at this point.

"My whole family has weird names. My sister's name is Jambo. My brother's name is Yo. Like, 'Yo, what's up?' Actually, he has the longest recorded name in New York City. It's Yo Xing Heyno Augustus Eisner Alexander Weiser Knuckles Alexander Jeremijenko-Conley. But one year he was like, 'Call me John.' And then he was like, 'Call me Dragon.' So, he went through his phases, but I never did.

"When I was little I didn't speak to anyone. In elementary school, I was best friends with a tree. Her name was Blossom. She's still there. I never realized how quiet I was because there was so much noise in my head.

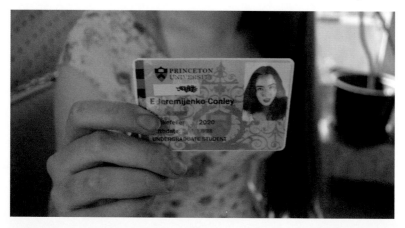

Then I made this conscious decision; I went to a new school in sixth grade and started talking. But that shyness never leaves you. There's still that tiny moment of fear, and you push through it. I think everyone's personality is a reaction to their personality as a child, whether it's the same—or for me—as an active dis tancing. I never stop talking now, but I might one day want to get back to the quiet girl.

"My name does a lot of the work when meeting new people. It's a good ice-breaker I get teased a lot by my friends because I always introduce myself: 'Hi, I'm E, like the letter.' Because otherwise people think my name is Eve for a month. But now I get the problem of them being like, 'Oh, your name's Elikcalctta?'

"A lot of people put the period after the E. In my college system they put a dot. People don't even think about it. It's like they have to. I had to go to the office and be like, 'Please take the dot off.'

"A lot of people meet me and say, 'You're the weirdest person I've ever met.' So, it's not really something I can control. I've never tried to Rebellion is very normal in my family. My parents were always like, 'Throw more parties! Wear shorter dresses!' But I don't drink, I've never cursed in my life. I actually have not yet had my first kiss. So, this is all like my secret rebellion."

40

"THE RISING SUN"
DIAMOND
DIAMOND DISTRICT, MANHATTAN
0.10 CARAT AND UP

For years, diamond cutter Zev Weitman toiled in
his cramped factory trying to find a new way to
cut a diamond to give it more sparkle. Depending
on his mood, the grandfather of eighteen
might compare his struggles to mathematician
John Nash in *A Beautiful Mind* or even Albert
Einstein's quest to discover $E = mc^2$.

When I first saw *A Beautiful Mind* I thought, 'This movie is for me.' I'm embarrassed to say . . . I have OCD, and he had the schizophrenia. I'm out of the box, and he was out of the box. He created an original theory about cooperation that won the Nobel Prize. Me? I'm looking to create the diamond with the best light performance.

"I killed myself for fourteen years to find it. I told my wife, 'I'm not coming home tonight. I'm sleeping in the factory.' Time is money, but I didn't care about money. When my daughter was little she used to say, 'Daddy, are you going to work on regular work so you can bring home a little bit of money, or are you going to be doing that other thing?'

"Albert Einstein sat there for twenty-five years trying to answer one question and ended up splitting the atom. Most people give up before that.

"I created a diamond I call The Rising Sun. I have a patent on it. You first have to understand Marcel Tolkowsky to understand my diamond. In 1919, Marcel Tolkowsky invented the round brilliant diamond cut. It's the modern day benchmark of diamond cutting. He figured out what the exact angles should be coming off of the top of the diamond.

"But even with a pivotal invention, who says that it's complete? Who says you can't add to it? You see, Tolkowsky wasn't changing the *arrangement* of the eight main facets of the diamond. He was subjecting them to the ideal angles that he discovered. My contribution is regarding the auxiliary facets. I added some and changed their shapes and rearranged them in order to put them *all* on ideal angles.

"A good metaphor for splitting facets is—think of a house. The foundation stays the same. The roof and the floors don't change, but you are moving rooms around and splitting rooms to let more light in. My diamond is like a sunburst. It has more light and texture and definition.

It has more brilliance and more fire. It has more everything. I mean, there's nothing that it's missing.

"I made the discovery in 2009. I spent all night and the next day in the factory, and that's when I saw this beautiful rising sun so clearly. I remember thinking, 'I'm rich! I don't have to worry about money anymore!'

"It's about 11:30 p.m., and I walk outside, and I see people jumping and screaming and going nuts. I thought, 'How the hell do they know what I just discovered?' It was New Year's Eve, and I had no idea. That's how disoriented I was.

"I'm an artist. I remember as a child making a statue of Abraham Lincoln from clay. Think about that. Now, I take a piece of rock and make a beautiful diamond. It's like sculpture. I love diamond cutting, but I don't make money doing it. I'm such a good cutter. People know. Without bragging, I make a beautiful job.

It has more brilliance and more fire.

"They pay me twice as much, but I work five times more. It doesn't work out. That's why I became a teacher. But the teaching stopped because somebody figured out how to cut diamonds overseas. The industry moved to India. When I came to this profession thirty-five years ago, there were three thousand cutters. Now there aren't even two hundred. I'm left only because I do repairs. I fix other people's mistakes.

"Now I have The Rising Sun. There are articles in science journals about my technique. They wrote that I am achieving more uniform light dispersion than the standard Round Brilliant cut. A diamond is a prism. All about angles and light performance. It's optical physics.

"Consumers see it with the naked eye. But first you have to create demand. Then supply. Is anybody looking for my new cut? No. You need to advertise first. I'm one guy with no money, and I'm against billionaires who don't want my diamonds coming into to the market.

"My friend said to me, 'You're going to make a lot of money. But you're not doing this for the money. You're just doing it for you.' And it's true. I just want to see the thing light up. I'm obsessed with it.

"I'll tell you what my mother once said about me, 'Let me tell you something about Zev. Everything that everybody else can do—he can't do. But what he *can* do—*nobody* else can do.'"

41

COMMON DUCKWEED (*LEMNA MINOR*)
AQUATIC PLANT
CENTRAL PARK, MANHATTAN

⅟₁₆ INCH

Naturalist Leslie Day has written several field guides about the nature, birds, and street trees of New York City. Ask her about her favorite petite plant in the five boroughs, and she'll be happy to enlighten you about what makes duckweed such a big deal.

I love duckweed. They are small floating plants that grow on still water. It is amazing that they're complete, flowering plants and yet they're so tiny. They have a stamen and pistil, which you can hardly see with the naked eye. They're the tiniest angiosperms in the world.

"Duckweed is highly nutritious. The waterfowl love them; fish will eat them. It's high in protein and carbohydrates. It's used for agricultural animal feed, treating wastewater, removing toxins from waterways, and may be a future source of ethanol for biofuel.

"When a duck or a heron is swimming around, the duckweed adheres to their legs, feathers, and beaks. They fly off to a different body of water, and the duckweed comes off when they land. That is the way it spreads.

"I was born on West 73rd Street. I always loved nature. I drew so many trees, the crayon called 'yellow green,' the color closest to early spring, was always used up first.

"Fast-forward. I read a book by Anaïs Nin about women who live in houseboats. That's why I decided to live on the water. I bought a

boat at the 79th Street Boat Basin for four thousand dollars, which I had to borrow.

"I really loved birds. I would walk around with a pocket full of seed. One day, this beautiful bird showed up with a red crest and beak. The next day it was there and the day after that. So I borrowed a field guide and looked it up. It was a female Northern Cardinal. She followed me for three years. At sunrise, she would sit on the railing along the Hudson and start calling to me. Then once, there was a blizzard. I was walking around the traffic circle on 79th Street, and out of the snow she flew to me, calling, calling, calling. I ran home and got the seed for her.

"One day this gorgeous red guy showed up. She took off with him. I never saw her again. Every time I'd see a female, I'd say, 'Is that you?' You know, they mate for life. She was such a wild and wonderful creature.

"She changed my life, because I went back to school. I wanted to know everything about nature. If it had a name, I wanted to know what it was—every living tree, flower, mushroom, fish, crab. I got my master's and my doctorate and started teaching science. This little bird was such an inspiration.

"Nature is so interesting, and it is so beautiful. Even if you're not interested in the science behind how plants grow, if you're only touched by the beauty, that's enough."

42

TRIPLE ZERO
KNITTING NEEDLE
TRAVIS, STATEN ISLAND
1¼ MILLIMETER

Little needle, big heart may not be an expression,
but when it comes to Tracy Gliaos, owner of the
The Naked Sheep yarn store, it is very much the
case. The expert knitter opened her shop so people
would have a place to knit and chat. But because
Gliaos has a serious talent not just for knitting
but also for listening, the place has turned into
something a lot bigger than a knitting store.

" A triple zero needle is the tiniest we have. The tiny needle is something you work up to. With this, you could do the tiniest little sock ever.

"The needle size has to do with the yarn thickness. When people start knitting, they start on a thick yarn because it's easier to manage, and they get the satisfaction of accomplishing something quickly.

The tiny needle is something you work up to.

"But when needles are small like this, you can make beautiful things, like a lace scarf. It does require more patience.

"When I was little, there was an English family that lived across the driveway from us, and the mom was teaching her daughters to knit crochet. I so wanted to do it. I was eight years old so I didn't have the dexterity and coordination, but I always remembered it.

"One day when I was about eighteen I decided it was time. I took some lessons at the local yarn store, and that was it.

"Years later, I was working for a corporation and all of a sudden I got pregnant at forty years old. The company was splitting up, and I was done with the corporate world anyway. My son was my priority. When he was three, I knew I had to do something but couldn't stomach the idea of going back to corporate.

"I'd been going to a shop in New Jersey with a big table where you can sit and knit. It felt homey. There wasn't a place in Staten Island where I felt comfortable knitting. One day I thought, 'I can do this. I'm going to open a knitting shop.'

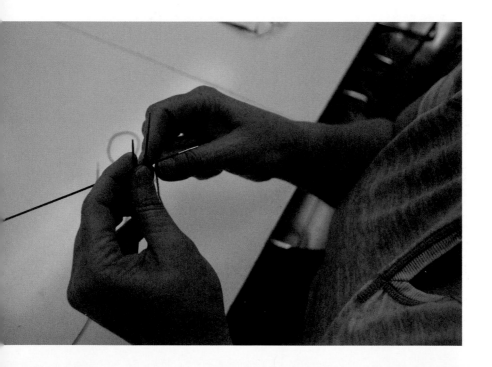

"People come in for a lot of different reasons. One woman who was just here lost her son, very young, in a tragic accident. She found her way back to wholeness through knitting. Another woman came in after she lost her mom. She'd been working on a piece, and when she was lost she would always call her mom. She came in broken and I said, 'OK, sit down. Let me see what you have. OK, this is how we're going to do it.'

"So we support one another. Somehow the idea of having people around the table to share your problems with, it becomes more than just, 'I dropped the stitch and how do I fix it?' It becomes, 'I'm having trouble with this piece. I feel like I'm dropping this stitch of my life, and help me fix it.'"

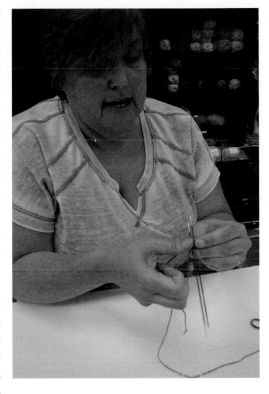

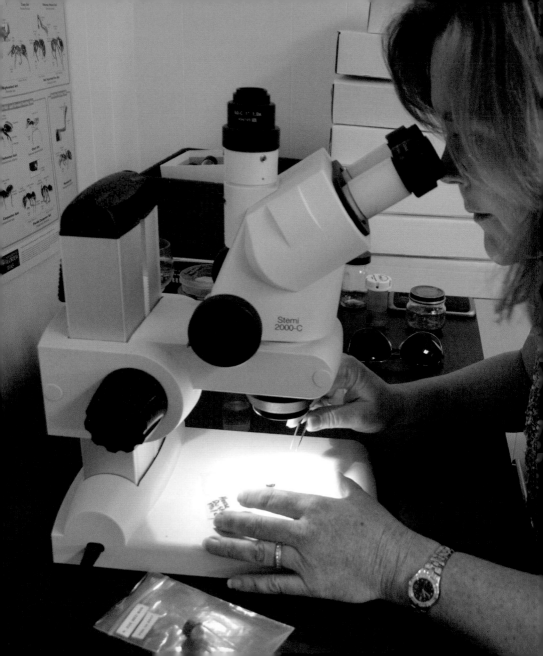

43

THRIPS
(ORDER: THYSANOPTERA)
PEST
NEW YORK CITY

1 MILLIMETER

Urban entomologist Jody Gangloff-Kaufmann is
in the business of managing pests—bedbugs,
dust mites, cockroaches, ticks, rats, mice, you
name it. But get her talking, and you'll
see she's got a soft spot for some hard-
to-see insects called thrips.

" I was always a biologist. I played in the dirt as a kid growing up on Long Island. I played with worms and mud and plants and butterflies and snakes. Anything. Everything.

"I got my PhD in entomology from Cornell. I ended up doing my thesis on thrips.

"If you look at a dandelion and you see a very tiny black insect wriggling, those are thrips. Onion farmers Upstate were pulling their hair out because thrips were resistant to pesticides. That's what my thesis was about.

"They have a sexual reproduction called Thelytoky. It's a Greek word. It's a type of parthenogenesis in which a female gives rise to another female without any males.

"The other thing that's cool is they have feather-like wings. They're so tiny the air is viscous for them so they kind of swim through the air.

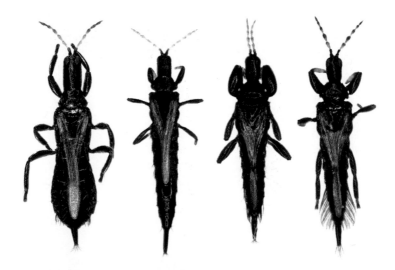

It's called a clap and fling flight mechanism. It's an adaptation. I just think they're cute.

"The truth is you eat a lot of insects. The tolerance for insect parts in food by the USDA is higher than you would imagine. For thrips in sauerkraut it's really high—like fifty thrips per 100 grams. They're so tiny they're not considered a contaminant.

"My work now is in community integrated pest management. Our focus is educating and helping the community. People call us with problems, and we answer the phone. They call about bedbugs, lawn-eating beetles, ticks, and so on.

"I was one of the first people to start working on bedbugs because New York City was the first place to have them. We started getting calls as early as 1997.

"I also studied rats. Columbus Park in Chinatown was loaded. They were just playing around in the bushes like squirrels.

"Dust mites are another problem. They live in the skin, scales, and debris that come off of humans and animals. The longer a home has existed, the bigger the issue can be. Some people in New York City have lived in their apartments for fifty years. The allergy dust mites cause for someone who has asthma can be very serious.

"Cockroaches carry diseases. They come up from the sewers so they carry bacteria. If they're in the kitchen, they can transmit disease. Their formal name is American cockroach but the Florida tourism name for them is Palmetto bug. It's like, 'Yes, it's just the Palmetto bug. Nothing to see here. Move along, as you were.'

"I think the fear of bugs is innate. Just like with rats and snakes. These creatures are dangerous. They can transmit disease. They can bite. They can sting. Our tendency to be frightened of things that are creepy-crawly makes total sense."

ABOUT THE AUTHOR

Suzi Siegel, who is little, grew up in a little apartment in the Bronx with very little distance between her window and the elevated Number 5 subway line.

While other little girls played with their three-story Barbie townhouses, she could amuse herself with a miniscule dust ball for hours on end. At the end of a long day investigating the tiny flotsam and jetsam of her household, Siegel would be carried to her bed. There, she forced herself to stay awake until she methodically recounted every word in her vocabulary.

Thus, she is uniquely qualified to write a book full of words about the tiny people, places, and things of New York City that might have otherwise gone unnoticed.

Her other credentials, which matter very little, are as follows: She has worked as a crime reporter in Detroit and an assistant to Sean "Diddy" Combs. She earned her master's degree from Harvard and has been to Djibouti. Her first concert was Ozzy Osbourne. Also, she once made out with Matt Dillon.